66 Days to Strategic Thinking

Pause. Think. Grow. Strategically.™

This journal is for anyone who has been told they aren't "strategic enough" or who wants to develop or strengthen their strategic mindset. Research shows it takes about 66 days to create a habit. In this journal, the pause isn't a separate stage; it's a discipline you'll practice every day.

Weekly 'Pause & Reflect' pages and a mid-journey checkpoint help you embed strategic pauses into your leadership life so that by the end of the program, pausing is no longer an event; it's part of who you are.

PAMELA J. GREEN, MBA, SPHR, PCC

Executive Coach · Leadership Strategist
· Creator of the Strategic Intelligence™ Framework

www.PamelaJGreen.com
www.MyStrategicIntelligence.com

66 Days to Strategic Thinking
Pause. Think. Grow. Strategically.™
Copyright © 2026 by Pamela J. Green
All rights reserved.

Published by Pamela J. Green Solutions, LLC
Bowie, MD
www.PamelaJGreen.com

IMPORTANT NOTE

This journal is intended for personal and professional development. It does not constitute legal, financial, medical, psychological, or therapeutic advice. Readers should consult appropriate professionals when making decisions requiring specialized expertise. The author and publisher disclaim liability for any actions taken based on this content.

INTELLECTUAL PROPERTY & COMMERCIAL USE RESTRICTIONS

This publication contains proprietary intellectual property, including but not limited to:

the Strategic Intelligence™ Framework; Strategic Intelligence Diagnostic™; Strategic Intelligence Decks™; ThinkSuite™ models; Pause–Think–Grow Strategically™ methodology; Strategic Intelligence system; and all assessments, prompts, exercises, and questions.

These materials may not be copied, adapted, excerpted, reproduced, or used in coaching, consulting, workshops, training programs, organizational development, licensed materials, or commercial applications without express written permission from the author.

INDIVIDUAL LICENSE ONLY

This journal is licensed solely for the personal use of the purchaser. It may not be shared, mass-copied, posted online, or distributed without a multi-user or organizational license.

AI & MACHINE LEARNING RESTRICTION

No portion of this publication may be used to train or feed artificial intelligence or machine-learning systems of any kind without written permission.

TRADEMARK NOTICES

ThinkSuite™, Pause. Think. Grow. Strategically.™, Strategic Intelligence Diagnostic™, Strategic Intelligence Decks™, and Strategic Intelligence™ are trademarks or pending trademarks owned by Pamela J. Green Solutions, LLC.

Published by Pamela J. Green Solutions, LLC

Bowie, MD

www.PamelaJGreen.com

Design & Layout: Diana Kosenko

Editor: Pamela J. Green Solutions, LLC

ISBN NUMBERS

Paperback ISBN   978-1-7371973-4-8
Hardcover ISBN   978-1-7371973-3-1
eBook ISBN   978-1-7371973-5-5

Printed in the United States of America

Contents

Welcome & Purpose

I'm so glad you're here.

I wish I'd had something like this when I was navigating my own years as a corporate and organizational leader and executive. Back then, I often longed for a space that would help me slow down, cut through the noise, and think more clearly, intentionally, and strategically. This journal is the resource I wish I'd been able to open each morning, a simple, structured way to build the habits of a true strategic thinker.

Today's world rewards speed and constant motion. But the challenges that really matter, the ones that shape people, teams, and entire organizations, don't yield to quick answers. They demand strategic thinking: the ability to pause, connect the dots, and anticipate impact before you act.

That's why this journey lasts 66 days. While popular wisdom has long claimed that new habits form in just 21 days, research led by health psychology scholar Phillippa Lally at University College London suggests a very different timeline. In a real-world study of everyday routines, Lally and her colleagues found that, on average, a new behavior required about 66 days of consistent practice before it felt automatic for participants (Lally, Van Jaarsveld, Potts, & Wardle, 2010). Building on this insight, this book invites you into a 66 day journey designed to transform strategic thinking from an occasional effort into a natural, nearly effortless part of how you approach your work and life. Two months of consistent practice can offer a powerful window for turning fresh insights into lasting habits.

Here's how we'll work together:

- **Daily action prompts** will help you exercise your "strategic thinking muscle."
- **Built-in pause cues** will nudge you to slow down and notice what really matters.
- **Reflection space** will capture the insights and patterns you discover along the way.

Consider inviting a trusted colleague, mentor, or coach to join you as an accountability partner. A short weekly check-in, perhaps just a five-minute call or a quick text, can keep you consistent and celebrate your progress. They might simply ask:

- "How consistently did you practice pausing and strategic thinking this week?"
- "What will you try that's unique, different, or better next week?"

My hope is that these pages become more than a journal. May they be a quiet place where you can hear your own wisdom, clarify what matters most, and grow into the kind of leader who sees possibilities others miss.

Welcome to **66 Days to Strategic Thinking**, let's pause, think, and grow together.

Pamela J. Green, MBA, SPHR, PCC,
Executive Coach and Leadership Strategist

What This Journal Is — and Is Not

This is not a productivity planner or a reflection notebook. It is a thinking discipline designed to help leaders make better decisions in complex environments.

How to Use This Journal

I designed this journal to be simple enough to fit into real life and strong enough to help you build the habit of thinking strategically every single day. Here's how to get the most from our 66 days together:

1. BEGIN WITH A BASELINE

Start by completing the **Strategic Intelligence Self-Assessment** that follows this section. It will help you see where you stand today in the ThinkSuite™ lenses of **Clarity, Confidence, and Impact**. Jot down one or two outcomes you hope to see by the end of these 66 days, this will be the picture you're moving toward.

2. CREATE A DAILY RHYTHM

Set aside **10–15 quiet minutes** each day. Consistency matters far more than perfection. If you miss a day, simply pick up where you left off.

Each daily page offers three parts:

- **Action Prompt** – a small, practical step to stretch your strategic thinking.
- **Pause Moment** – a short cue to stop, breathe, and notice what deserves your attention.
- **Reflection Space** – room to capture insights, wins, and next steps.

3. EMBRACE THE STRATEGIC CHALLENGE & ANCHOR

At the end of each week, you'll find a multi-page Strategic Challenge & Weekly Anchor. Use it to capture the bigger lessons: What surprised you? Where did your thinking deepen? What decisions or ideas need to be carried forward? These weekly pauses are the heartbeat of the journal; they turn daily actions into insight.

4. INVITE AN ACCOUNTABILITY PARTNER

Growth sticks when someone walks the journey with you. Choose a trusted colleague, mentor, or coach, and set up a short weekly check-in, a five-minute call, or even a simple text exchange works beautifully.

They might ask:

- "How consistently did you practice pausing and strategic thinking this week?"
- "What will you do that's unique, different, or better in the coming week?"

A gentle nudge like this keeps your commitments visible and your progress measurable.

5. SCAN THE HORIZON

The most successful leaders make a daily practice of scanning the horizon, reading widely, seeking diverse perspectives, and exposing themselves to insights that stretch their thinking. Strategic leaders don't wait for clarity to arrive; they actively create it. They read, listen, watch, and observe because they know that new information is the raw material of strategic intelligence.

Daily, I'll invite you to adopt a daily habit of scanning the horizon to break out of the narrow view of today's tasks and step into a wider lens, one shaped by trends, patterns, innovations, and early signals that others miss. This simple habit expands your imagination, strengthens your foresight, and accelerates your growth as a strategic thinker.

a. Warren Buffett (Investor & CEO)

- Reads 5–6 hours a day: financial reports, newspapers, books.
- Says reading is the key to compounding knowledge.

b. Indra Nooyi (Former CEO, PepsiCo)

- Constantly scanned trends across industries, cultures, and technologies.
- Says leaders "must refresh what they know" weekly.

c. Bill Gates (Microsoft Co-Founder)

- Reads 50+ books per year.
- Blocks "Think Weeks" for uninterrupted reading and horizon scanning.

d. Ursula Burns (Former CEO, Xerox)

- Credits reading widely and seeking cross-industry insights as essential to her rise.

6. CELEBRATE THE MILESTONE

Habit research shows it takes about 66 days for a new behavior to feel natural (Lally, van Jaarsveld, Potts, & Wardle, 2009, European Journal of Social Psychology). On Day 66, you'll find an extended check-in to review your journey, celebrate what you've built, and plan how to sustain and scale your new habits.

This isn't just a notebook; it's a practice. Show up each day, pause intentionally, and let these pages help you become the kind of strategic thinker who sees possibilities others miss.

Strategic Intelligence Self-Assessment

Complete before **Day 1** and revisit on **Day 66** to measure your growth as a strategic thinker.

INSTRUCTIONS

For each statement below, rate how true it is for you **today**:

1 = Not true   **3** = Occasionally true   **5** = Very true

2 = Seldom true   **4** = Often true

LENS 1: CLARITY – Seeing the Big Picture

1. I deliberately step back to understand the broader context before making decisions.
2. I connect daily actions to my long-term goals and organizational strategy.
3. I can clearly explain the trends, forces, or data shaping my environment.
4. I look beyond immediate problems to uncover underlying patterns.
5. I regularly pause to test whether my work aligns with the outcomes that matter most.

LENS 2: CONFIDENCE – Thinking Boldly and Deciding with Courage

1. I make decisions even when information is incomplete or ambiguous.
2. I trust my ability to weigh options and anticipate second-order effects.
3. I invite diverse viewpoints, then confidently synthesize them into a clear direction.
4. I stay grounded and composed when strategic choices carry high stakes.
5. I recover quickly when a decision doesn't play out as expected and adjust with focus.

1. I translate strategic ideas into concrete actions that move key priorities forward.
2. I influence stakeholders outside my immediate team or department.
3. I build alliances that help execute long-range plans.
4. I can point to outcomes that reflect thoughtful, forward-looking decisions.
5. I mentor or coach others to strengthen their own strategic thinking.

SCORING & REFLECTION

- Add the scores for each lens (range 5–25).
- Identify the lens with your lowest total; this is your primary growth area for the next 66 days.
- After rating yourself, jot down:
  - Where do I already think and act strategically?
  - Where do I get pulled back into short-term or reactive thinking?
  - What single shift would most improve my strategic thinking in the months ahead?

STRATEGIC TIP: Repeat this assessment on **Day 66** and compare it to your starting scores. Notice where your clarity, confidence, and impact as a strategic thinker have grown.

Why the Pause Matters

Great leaders are often rewarded for speed, quick decisions, fast pivots, and constant action. Yet the very complexity of today's environment demands the opposite: intentional pauses that create space for strategic thinking.

A pause is not a retreat from action; it is a **strategic discipline**.

It allows you to:

Gain Clarity	Strengthen Confidence	Maximize Impact
Step back from the noise to reconnect with your purpose and the bigger picture.	Create the mental space to weigh options, anticipate consequences, and trust your judgment.	Ensure that your next move aligns with your executive brand and produces results that matter.

In the **Think Like a Brand** series, the pause is described as the "white space" where insight happens. In ThinkSuite™, it is the deliberate moment that transforms **reaction** into **intelligent action**.

How to Incorporate the Pause in Your Leadership Life

1. SCHEDULE MICRO-PAUSES

- Block 5–10 minutes between major meetings.
- Use these breaks to jot a quick reflection: *What truly needs my attention next?*

2. ANCHOR TO DAILY ROUTINES

Pair a pause with something you already do, such as your morning coffee, a midday walk, or the end-of-day review. Consistency is what creates a habit.

3. PRACTICE "STRATEGIC SILENCE"

Before responding to a complex issue or high-stakes question, count a slow five or take two to five deep breaths. Give your brain the time it needs to think strategically.

4. CREATE A WEEKLY "THINK HOUR"

Reserve one uninterrupted hour each week to step back from operations. Review goals, revisit priorities, and capture insights. Guard it like any other key meeting.

5. JOURNAL WITH INTENTION

Use the daily prompts in this journal as built-in pauses. Writing clarifies thinking and reveals patterns you might otherwise miss.

6. MODEL THE PAUSE FOR YOUR TEAM

Share your practice openly, "I'm taking a moment to think this through." This normalizes reflection and encourages others to do the same.

REFLECTION PROMPT

Where will you place your first intentional pause this week? Please write it down now and treat it as an unmissable leadership appointment.

....

....

....

....

....

....

In Case You Fall Off

Because you will, and that's part of the strategic journey.

- Strategic thinking isn't about perfection.
- It's about returning with intention.

Over the next 66 days, there will be days when you lose focus, get overwhelmed, or forget to complete your practice. That isn't failure, it's evidence that you're human. What matters most is how quickly and compassionately you get back on track. Self-compassion is a very important part of this journey. It enables your quick recovery and your ability to correct your course when needed.

This page offers a simple, 5-minute reset ritual to regain your momentum whenever you drift.

Before you begin this 66-day journey, it's important to understand something that most traditional goal-setting systems don't tell you:

You will fall off.
You will miss a day.
You will get overwhelmed.
You will forget.
You will have mornings where your motivation is low or your schedule is packed.

This isn't a flaw in your character. It's not a sign that you can't be consistent. It's not proof that you're "not disciplined." It is simply how the human brain works.

Strategic thinking is not built through flawless performance. It's built through intentional return; the ability to reset, refocus, and realign quickly when life gets busy.

Over the next 66 days, you are strengthening three critical leadership muscles:

1. SELF-AWARENESS

Recognizing when you've drifted, without judgment.

2. SELF-REGULATION

Interrupting old patterns and choosing a new response.

3. STRATEGIC DISCIPLINE

Returning to your plan with clarity instead of shame. Leaders don't lose momentum because they drift. They lose momentum because they let the drift define them.

- This page is your safety net.
- Your permission slip.
- Your reset button.

Anytime you fall off track, and you will, use the 5-Minute Strategic Reset on this page to reenter the journey with intention.

- **You are not starting over.**
- **You are starting again, stronger than before.**

The 5-Minute Strategic Reset

When you notice you've fallen off, whether it's one day or ten, pause and walk through these five questions:

1. WHAT SLIPPED?

(Without judgment. Just name it.)

2. WHAT'S CURRENTLY STUCK OR OVERDUE?

(This is how you strengthen your ability to get and remain clear-headed)

3. WHAT MATTERS MOST RIGHT NOW?

(Choose one priority for the next 24–48 hours.)

4. WHAT IS ONE SMALL ACTION I CAN TAKE TODAY?

(Action restores clarity.)

5. WHAT SUPPORT OR ADJUSTMENT DO I NEED?

(Strategic thinkers don't rely on willpower alone.)

REMEMBER THIS

Consistency is built through returning, not perfection. Every time you reset, you strengthen your strategic mindset.

- You are not starting over.
- You are starting again, with more insight than before.

66-Day Accountability Overview

A simple structure to help you stay consistent, intentional, and strategic.

Strategic thinking is not built through intensity, it's built through consistent, intentional practice. This 66-Day Accountability System gives you a predictable rhythm to follow, so you always know how to move forward, reset, and stay aligned with your long-term goals.

Think of this page as your roadmap, your support system, and your re-entry point whenever the journey feels challenging.

The Accountability System at a Glance

This journey is supported by four simple components:

1. YOUR DAILY STRATEGIC PRACTICE

Every day, you'll complete a short, focused reflection and strategic action. These daily pages are the foundation of your consistency and clarity.

DAILY ROUTINE INCLUDES:

- A brief reflection
- A single strategic action
- A micro-moment of clarity or intention

This keeps you grounded and moving forward one step at a time.

2. YOUR WEEKLY STRATEGIC ANCHOR

Once each week, you will complete the **Weekly Strategic Anchor Page**, a 5–10 minute ritual that resets your focus and reinforces your strategic priorities.

YOUR ANCHOR INCLUDES:

- A review of wins
- Identification of what's stuck

- Top 3 priorities
- One strategic action for the week
- Support or resources needed

Choose a **consistent day & time** for your Weekly Strategic Anchor. Consistency creates momentum.

3. THE 5-MINUTE STRATEGIC RESET

Life will get busy. You will fall behind. This is normal and expected.

Whenever you drift, use the **In Case You Fall Off** page to reenter the journey without guilt or pressure. The reset helps you:

- Name the slip
- Regain clarity
- Choose a small next step
- Reconnect to your purpose

Strategic thinkers don't avoid drift, they recover quickly from it.

4. YOUR 66-DAY STRATEGIC REVIEW

At the end of the journey, you'll complete the **66-Day Review Page** to capture your transformation.

This powerful reflection helps you:

- Identify patterns
- Evaluate what worked
- Celebrate progress
- Clarify your new strategic identity
- Choose your next commitment

This becomes the foundation of your next 66 days and your next level of leadership.

Your Personal Accountability Plan

Use the prompts below to define how you will stay committed to your 66-day journey:

MY PURPOSE FOR THESE 66 DAYS:

MY DAILY COMMITMENT:
(When will you complete your daily practice?)

MY WEEKLY STRATEGIC ANCHOR DAY & TIME:

WHO WILL SUPPORT OR CHEER ME ON (OPTIONAL):
(Names, roles, or simply "my future self.")

WHAT I WILL DO WHEN I FALL OFF:

My Accountability Promise

Write out the promise in the space below and then initial or sign it as your commitment to yourself:

"For the next 66 days, I commit to showing up with intention, not perfection."

Signature/Initial   Date

The 66-Day Strategic Thinking Roadmap

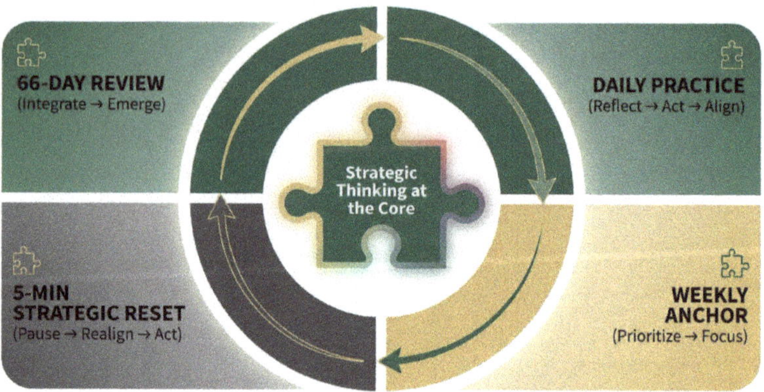

PHASE 1: FOUNDATIONS (DAYS 1–21)

- Future Focus
- Horizon Scanning
- Strategic Questions

PHASE 2: APPLICATION (DAYS 22–42)

- Alignment
- Systems Thinking
- Trade-offs

PHASE 3: INTEGRATION (DAYS 43–63)

- Pattern Recognition
- Scenario Thinking
- Influence & Communication

PHASE 4: MASTERY & INTEGRATION (DAYS 64–66)

END OF THE DAY CHECK-IN: WHY EACH WORD MATTERS

These five words were chosen deliberately; each represents a distinct state of mind that often arises when someone is practicing strategic thinking. They provide a quick, low-effort way to capture the quality of your day, eliminating the need for a lengthy reflection.

CLEAR

Signals: mental clarity, confidence, a sense that priorities and next steps are understood.

Why it's here: Strategic thinking often aims for clarity of purpose and action.

CURIOUS

Signals: openness, questions, willingness to explore.

Why it's here: Curiosity is a core driver of strategic insight; it shows you are scanning for new possibilities.

STRETCHED

Signals: you were challenged, perhaps outside your comfort zone.

Why it's here: Growth and strategic capability come when we operate at the edge of our usual patterns.

UNSURE

Signals: ambiguity, uncertainty, not yet seeing the whole picture.

Why it's here: Strategic work is often messy; noticing uncertainty is part of learning to pause and think before acting.

ENERGIZED

Signals: motivation, excitement, renewed commitment.

Why it's here: When strategic thinking connects to purpose, it often leaves us feeling recharged.

HOW THEY WORK TOGETHER

- The set covers a spectrum: from clarity and excitement to challenge and ambiguity.

- None of the words is "good" or "bad," each captures a different strategic thinking state.
- Circling a word each evening provides a quick emotional snapshot and helps you see patterns over the 66 days (for example, noticing when "Curious" shows up more frequently, or when "Unsure" signals areas needing more reflection).

EXPECTED OUTCOME AFTER 66 DAYS

- You pause before reacting, connecting daily work to bigger goals.
- You naturally use more "why this matters long-term" language.
- Strategic thinking is no longer an event, it's a habit.

Phase 1 – Foundations (Days 1-21)

When I began my leadership career, I often felt pulled in a dozen directions, reacting to the urgent rather than shaping the important. My tendency to rely on inefficient thinking patterns when addressing complex challenges was not effective. I needed a way to shift into higher-order thinking, and I wish someone had handed me a simple practice to help me *pause, think,* and grow into a more strategic thinker and leader.

These first three weeks are that practice. We'll build the mental muscles that every strategic thinker relies on:

Future Focus	Strategic Curiosity	Intentional Pause
Lifting your gaze beyond today's tasks to see the long-term horizon.	Asking better questions before rushing to answers.	Creating space to notice what truly matters.

The brain rewires through repetition. Strategic thinking becomes easier, faster, and more automatic the more it is practiced. Over time, the brain requires less effort to access these pathways, making the behavior more automatic and reliable.

This is why insight alone rarely leads to change. Strategic thinking is not a one-time realization, it is a practice. Repeated, intentional thinking reshapes how leaders notice patterns, test assumptions, and make decisions, especially under pressure.

The 66-day structure is designed to work with the brain, not against it. Through consistent, small acts of reflection and choice, new thinking pathways are reinforced until strategic thinking becomes a default response rather than a deliberate effort.

Strategic capacity is not built through intensity; it is built through repetition.

In roughly 66 days, a consistent practice can become a habit. These first 21 days lay the groundwork and are your "warm-up set." By the end of this phase, you'll notice yourself naturally asking, *"How does today shape tomorrow?"* and permitting yourself to pause before reacting.

> *The illiterate of the 21st century will not be those who cannot read, but those who cannot learn, unlearn, and relearn.*
>
> -ALVIN TOFFLER

Day 1 — Future Focus

Train your mind to step out of the urgent and into the intentional by looking at today's work through a long-term lens.

MORNING PROMPT   (~5 MIN)

Before the day takes off, pause and write below:

"What's the one decision or action today that matters most for the long-term success of my team or organization?"

Be specific. Name the decision or action and why it matters. This builds the habit of starting the day with a future-focused priority.

SCAN THE HORIZON   (~5–10 MIN)

Read or listen to one short piece outside your immediate field, a news article, an industry trend, a leadership blog, or a technology brief. Jot a quick note: **What insight or trend caught my attention?** This stretches your perspective beyond today's to-do list.

ASK A STRATEGIC QUESTION   (~5 MIN)

Choose one area of your work and ask:

- What does success look like in one year?
- What might get in our way?
- What's a possible unintended consequence?

Capture the question and your first thoughts. The aim isn't a perfect answer, but to strengthen foresight.

A brief, intentional pause used to test whether a decision advances long-term direction rather than short-term urgency.

For every meaningful decision you make, pause briefly:

"Does this align with where we want to be in 1–3 years?"

A simple yes/no note is enough. This links daily choices to bigger goals.

END-OF-DAY CHECK

Circle or underline the word below that best captures your mindset tonight:

Clear   Curious   Stretched   Unsure   Energized

STRATEGIC TIP: If you circled *Curious* or *Unsure*, list one resource, an article, a mentor, a short video, you'll explore to help you move toward clarity.

....

....

In a sentence or two, finish:

Today I noticed:
....

....

....

and

Tomorrow I will:
....

....

....

WHY IT MATTERS

Strategic thinkers make a habit of lifting their gaze beyond the immediate. Starting each morning with a long-term question, and ending with a quick reflection, trains your brain to connect today's actions to tomorrow's success.

Day 2 — Future Focus

Strengthen your habit of scanning the horizon so you can see beyond today's urgent tasks.

MORNING PROMPT (~5 MIN)

Pause and write:

"What trend, idea, or conversation from yesterday could shape our success one year from now?"

It could be something you read, a comment from a colleague, or even a shift you sense in your industry.

SCAN THE HORIZON (~5–10 MIN)

Find one article, podcast clip, or short video outside your immediate field (economics, technology, social trends, science, or art). Jot a quick note: **What insight or question does this raise for our work?**

ASK A STRATEGIC QUESTION (~5 MIN)

Choose a current project or decision and ask:

"If this were wildly successful in three years, what would have to be true?"

Write your first thoughts, don't edit for feasibility; capture possibilities.

When you face a meaningful decision, pause:

"Does this move us closer to where we want to be in 1–3 years?"

A simple yes/no note, or a few words on why, keeps you linking action to long-term goals.

END-OF-DAY CHECK

Circle the word that best fits your mindset tonight:

Clear   Curious   Stretched   Unsure   Energized

STRATEGIC TIP: If you circled *Curious* or *Unsure*, list one resource, an article, a mentor, a short video, you'll explore to help you move toward clarity.

In a sentence or two, finish:

Today I noticed:

and

Tomorrow I will:

WHY IT MATTERS

Strategic thinkers don't just react to the news they connect emerging signals to future decisions. Today's exercise strengthens your ability to spot trends early and imagine how they might influence the path ahead.

Day 3 — Future Focus

GOAL

Practice connecting today's conversations and choices to the bigger picture so long-term thinking becomes second nature.

MORNING PROMPT (~5 MIN)

Pause and write:

"Which decision or conversation today, if handled well, could have the greatest impact a year from now?"

Name the decision or conversation. Note why it matters to your team or organization's long-term success.

....

....

SCAN THE HORIZON (~5–10 MIN)

Read, watch, or listen to one piece of content outside your immediate field, for example, a technology article, a cultural trend report, or a global economic update. Jot a sentence or two: **What opportunity or risk might this signal for us in the next 12–36 months?**

....

....

ASK A STRATEGIC QUESTION (~5 MIN)

Pick a current initiative and ask:

"If nothing changes in our environment over the next year, what risk might we be overlooking?"

Capture your first thoughts, don't overthink. This question trains you to look for blind spots.

....

....

....

When you face a meaningful decision, pause briefly:

"Does this action keep us aligned with where we want to be in 1–3 years?"

Record a quick yes/no or a phrase that captures your reasoning.

END-OF-DAY CHECK

Circle the word that best matches your mindset tonight:

Clear   Curious   Stretched   Unsure   Energized

STRATEGIC TIP: If you circled *Curious* or *Unsure*, list one resource, an article, a mentor, a short video, you'll explore to help you move toward clarity.

Complete the sentences:

Today I noticed:

and

Tomorrow I will:

WHY IT MATTERS

Great strategic thinkers don't just react; they anticipate what could be missed. Today's exercise strengthens your ability to uncover hidden risks and keep long-term priorities front and center.

Day 4 — Future Focus

Strengthen the habit of looking beyond today's tasks to anticipate what tomorrow may require.

MORNING PROMPT (~5 MIN)

Pause and write:

"What conversation or decision today could influence our success three years from now, and what one question will I ask to keep that conversation future-focused?"

Identify the decision or conversation and draft the question you'll ask to help everyone look ahead.

SCAN THE HORIZON (~5–10 MIN)

Choose a short piece of content outside your usual field, for example, a scientific breakthrough, a public-policy update, or a trend in consumer behavior.

Note: **What possibility or risk does this raise for my work or organization in the next 12–36 months?**

ASK A STRATEGIC QUESTION (~5 MIN)

For a current project or issue, ask:

"If our environment changes dramatically in the next year, what opportunities could appear that we haven't planned for?"

Jot the first ideas that surface, don't edit or overanalyze.

When a meaningful decision crosses your desk, pause briefly:

"Does this move us closer to where we want to be in 1–3 years?"

Capture a quick yes/no or a few words on why.

....

END-OF-DAY CHECK

Circle the word that best describes your mindset tonight:

Clear   Curious   Stretched   Unsure   Energized

STRATEGIC TIP: If you circled *Curious* or *Unsure*, list one resource, an article, a mentor, a short video, you'll explore to help you move toward clarity.

....

Complete the sentences:

Today I noticed:
....

....

....

and

Tomorrow I will:
....

....

....

WHY IT MATTERS

Strategic thinkers practice stretching the time horizon every day. By intentionally asking forward-looking questions and scanning unfamiliar territory, you build the reflex to spot opportunities and risks before they surface.

Day 5 — Future Focus

GOAL

Deepen your practice of spotting early signals that can influence long-term success.

MORNING PROMPT (~5 MIN)

Pause and write:

"What early sign, inside or outside my organization, could indicate the direction of our industry a year from now?"

Consider a subtle indicator, such as a customer request, a policy discussion, a new technology, or a social trend.

SCAN THE HORIZON (~5–10 MIN)

Read, watch, or listen to one piece of content outside your immediate role, perhaps a global market update, an innovation story, or an article about emerging social behavior.

Note in a sentence or two: **What signal or pattern stood out?** Ask yourself: **How might this influence our strategy in the next 12–36 months?**

ASK A STRATEGIC QUESTION (~5 MIN)

Choose a current initiative and ask:

"If this initiative succeeds beyond expectations, what will we need to have in place to sustain it?"

Capture your first thoughts without worrying about polish.

When you face a meaningful decision, pause briefly and consider:

"Does this move us closer to where we want to be in 1–3 years?"

Record a quick yes/no or a phrase that captures your reasoning.

END-OF-DAY CHECK

Circle the word that best describes your mindset tonight:

Clear   Curious   Stretched   Unsure   Energized

STRATEGIC TIP: If you circled *Curious* or *Unsure*, list one resource, an article, a mentor, a short video, you'll explore to help you move toward clarity.

Complete the sentences:
Today I noticed:

and
Tomorrow I will:

WHY IT MATTERS

Strategic thinkers look for **weak signals**, early indicators that a shift is coming, so they can prepare before the trend is obvious. Today's practice builds the reflex to notice those subtle cues and connect them to long-term goals.

Day 6 — Future Focus

Sharpen your ability to connect today's choices with tomorrow's possibilities by noticing long-term implications in everyday work.

MORNING PROMPT (~5 MIN)

Pause and write:

"Which project or conversation today (if successful) could create opportunities we haven't even imagined yet?"

Name the project or conversation and briefly describe the opportunity you think it might unlock.

SCAN THE HORIZON (~5–10 MIN)

Choose a short article, podcast, or video outside your usual field, for example, a piece on emerging technology, demographic shifts, or a global trend.

Note in a sentence or two: **What potential opportunity or risk could this signal for us over the next 12–36 months?**

ASK A STRATEGIC QUESTION (~5 MIN)

Select a current decision or initiative and ask:

"If we do nothing differently for the next year, what unintended consequences might arise?"

Write your first thoughts, don't edit or overthink.

When you face a meaningful decision, pause briefly:

"Does this action move us closer to where we want to be in 1–3 years?"

Record a quick yes/no or a few words to capture your reasoning.

....

END-OF-DAY CHECK

Circle the word that best describes your mindset tonight:

Clear   Curious   Stretched   Unsure   Energized

STRATEGIC TIP: If you circled *Curious* or *Unsure*, list one resource, an article, a mentor, a short video, you'll explore to help you move toward clarity.

....

Finish each sentence:

Today I noticed:
....

....

....

and

Tomorrow I will:
....

....

....

WHY IT MATTERS

Strategic thinkers spot the second- and third-order effects of their choices. Today's practice trains you to anticipate the ripple effects of inaction or delayed decisions, an essential skill for leading in complex environments.

Day 7 — Future Focus

End your first week by gathering insights and spotting patterns in what you've noticed so far.

MORNING PROMPT (~5 MIN)

Pause and write:

"Looking back over the past six days, what long-term opportunities or risks are starting to come into focus?"

List two or three that stand out, even if they're only early signals.

SCAN THE HORIZON (~5–10 MIN)

Choose one short article, podcast, or video outside your normal field, it might be a cultural trend, a new technology, or a global economic update.

Jot a quick note: **What did I learn that could shape our strategy in the next 1–3 years?**

ASK A STRATEGIC QUESTION (~5 MIN)

Pick a current initiative and ask:

"If this initiative were to exceed expectations, what new challenges might we face a year from now?"

Capture your first thoughts without editing.

When you face a meaningful decision, pause briefly:

"Does this move us closer to where we want to be in 1–3 years?"

Write a short yes/no or a phrase explaining why.

END-OF-DAY CHECK

Circle the word that best describes your mindset tonight:

Clear   Curious   Stretched   Unsure   Energized

STRATEGIC TIP: If you circled *Curious* or *Unsure*, list one resource, an article, a mentor, a short video, you'll explore to help you move toward clarity.

Complete each sentence:

Today I noticed:

and

Tomorrow I will:

WHY IT MATTERS

Strategic thinking grows stronger when you pause to connect the dots. Today's reflection helps you see the patterns emerging from your first week of practice and prepares you for the next phase.

This Week's Strategic Challenge – Week 1: Future Focus

Your board is excited about a fast-moving opportunity that promises a quick revenue bump.

Pursuing it would divert people and budget from the three-year strategic plan you helped create.

1. Identify the long-term outcomes you most want to protect.

2. Draft two or three clarifying questions you would ask the board before making a decision.

3. Capture the single action you would take next, and why, to keep the organization future-focused.

- How does your usual instinct compare to the action you chose after pausing?
- What did this exercise reveal about how you balance short-term gains with long-term strategy?

Explore additional scenarios and companion resources designed to deepen your use of the *ThinkSuite™ Strategic Intelligence Decks™*. Visit **www.pamelajgreen.com/store** for details.

Weekly Strategic Anchor

A Rhythm That Protects Your Progress

Strategic thinking isn't sustained by motivation it's sustained by rhythm. Your Weekly Strategic Anchor is the one consistent ritual that keeps your goals, your focus, and your decisions aligned throughout the 66-day journey.

PURPOSE OF THE WEEKLY STRATEGIC ANCHOR

- Reconnect to your strategic priorities
- Review progress without judgment
- Anticipate obstacles before they derail you
- Recommit to the habits that matter most
- Make small adjustments that protect your long-term goals

Your anchor keeps you from drifting too far from your intentions, even during busy or overwhelming weeks.

YOUR WEEKLY STRATEGIC ANCHOR RITUAL

Complete this every week on the same day, at the same time. Choose a moment that feels calm, available, and repeatable.

My Weekly Strategic Anchor Day & Time:

....

1. Strategic Wins This Week

What moved forward? What worked? List 2–3 wins, no matter how small.

....

....

2. What's Stuck or Slipping?

Identify challenges without blame. Awareness is your strategic leverage.

....

....

3. What Truly Mattered Most This Week?

Reflect on where your time, energy, and attention actually went.

The Three Priorities That Mattered Most:

1.

2.

3.

4. One Strategic Action for the Next 24 Hours

Choose the smallest meaningful action that moves your priority forward.

My One Action:

5. What Support or Resources Do I Need?

Strategic thinkers don't do it alone.

6. Alignment Check

Are my actions aligned with my long-term goals and values?

☐ Yes, keep going

☐ Not fully, what adjustment do I need to make?

Adjustment Needed (if any):

STRATEGIC INTEGRATION

"What does the strategic version of me need next week?"

Write your answer in one clear sentence:

PAUSE: When Overwhelm Blocks Strategic Thought

Strategic thinking rarely fails because of a lack of intelligence. More often, it fails because the mind is overloaded, not because your ability to think strategically is unavailable.

Before you move forward, take a moment to pause and reset your cognitive space. This brief reflection is designed to help you recognize, and reduce, the mental friction that keeps you from thinking strategically. Do this as often as is needed.

WHY YOU'RE FEELING OVERWHELMED

Overwhelm is simply a signal that your mental bandwidth has exceeded its limit. It is not a sign of weakness or inability.

Most overwhelm falls into one of three categories:

1. Volume Overwhelm

There is *too much*. Too many tasks, too many decisions, too many expectations.

2. Velocity Overwhelm

Things are coming *too fast*. You're responding more than you are leading.

3. Vagueness Overwhelm

There is not enough clarity. When expectations are unclear, the brain fills the gaps with worry, assumptions, or imagined consequences.

Identifying which type of overwhelm you're experiencing gives you the power to resolve it.

YOUR STRATEGIC RESET

Use this moment to shrink the problem and reclaim your mental space.

Ask yourself:

1. *Which type of overwhelm am I experiencing, Volume, Velocity, or Vagueness?*

2. *If I could remove just one pressure point, which one would have the greatest impact on my clarity?*

3. *What needs to become simpler? What needs to slow down? What needs to become clearer?*

These questions shift your brain out of emotional reactivity and back into strategic capacity.

MINI-EXERCISE: REDUCE THE LOAD

Choose one method below to immediately lighten your cognitive burden:

- **Three-Column Sort:**
  List your current responsibilities under
  Must Do / Should Do / Could Do
- **The 90-Day Filter:**
  Circle only what truly matters in the next 90 days.
- **Cynefin Cue:**
  Identify what is *simple*, what is *complicated*, and what is *complex*, and treat each accordingly.

Your goal is not to finish everything. Your goal is to create space for clear, strategic thought.

RECLAIM YOUR AGENCY

Overwhelm often makes you feel powerless. End this pause with a simple decision:

What is one small, strategic action I can take in the next 24 hours that will help me feel more in control?

1. Write it down.
2. Commit to it.
3. Let it become the next puzzle piece in your growth.

PAUSE. THINK. GROW. STRATEGICALLY.™

Your thinking expands when your mind has room to breathe. Use this pause any time you feel cognitive clutter rising or when your momentum begins to stall. Strategic thinking requires clarity, and clarity begins with space.

Welcome to Week 2

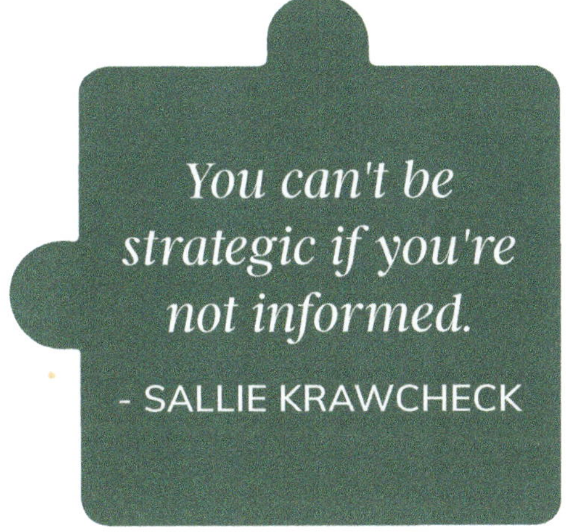

Day 8 — Horizon Scanning

Broaden your perspective by deliberately looking outside your usual sources of information.

MORNING PROMPT (~5 MIN)

Pause and write your answer to the prompt below:

"Where might a shift outside my organization, technology, culture, economy, or environment, create opportunities or risks in the next 12–36 months?"

List one or two possibilities that come to mind, even if they feel uncertain.

SCAN THE HORIZON (~5–10 MIN)

Find one article, podcast, video, or research brief well outside your daily responsibilities, for example:

- a breakthrough in science or medicine,
- a demographic or cultural trend,
- a new policy or regulatory change.

Note in a sentence or two: *What signal or insight could this send about the future of our field or organization?*

ASK A STRATEGIC QUESTION (~5 MIN)

Choose a current initiative and ask:

"If this external trend accelerates faster than expected, how might it change our strategy?"

Capture your first thoughts, don't worry about being right; you're training your mind to think ahead.

When you face a meaningful decision, pause briefly:

"Does this choice keep us aligned with where we want to be in 1–3 years?"

Record a quick yes/no or a few words explaining your reasoning.

....

END-OF-DAY CHECK

Circle the word that best fits your mindset tonight:

Clear   **Curious**   **Stretched**   **Unsure**   **Energized**

STRATEGIC TIP: If you circled *Curious* or *Unsure*, list one resource, an article, a mentor, a short video, you'll explore to help you move toward clarity.

Puzzle Piece	Fillable Statement
	I felt
	today because
	Before deciding what's next, I may need to
	(read, watch, ask, or reflect) to gain clarity.
	If you already know the next step, add:
	When I have that clarity, tomorrow I will

WHY IT MATTERS

Strategic thinkers **intentionally look beyond their own walls.** By scanning the horizon every day, you start to notice weak signals and emerging trends early, often long before they become obvious to others. This habit turns "future thinking" into a daily reflex.

Day 9 — Horizon Scanning

Strengthen your ability to spot early signals and imagine how they could reshape your strategy.

MORNING PROMPT   (~5 MIN)

Pause and write your response to the prompt below:

"What external shift, economic, technological, cultural, or environmental, could influence my organization's priorities within the next 1–3 years?"

List at least one possibility, even if you're unsure of its likelihood.

SCAN THE HORIZON   (~5–10 MIN)

Read, watch, or listen to one source beyond your normal field, for example:

- a global economic forecast,
- a breakthrough in science or AI,
- a trend report on consumer behavior.

Jot a brief note: What signal or pattern stands out, and how might it affect our strategy or decisions in the next few years?

ASK A STRATEGIC QUESTION   (~5 MIN)

Select a current project or decision and ask:

"If this outside trend accelerates faster than expected, what new risks or opportunities would appear?"

Write your first thoughts, this isn't about certainty, but about practicing foresight.

When a meaningful decision arises, pause:

"Does this action keep us aligned with where we want to be in 1–3 years?"

Record a quick yes/no or a few words capturing your reasoning.

END-OF-DAY CHECK

Circle the word that best matches your mindset tonight:

Clear   Curious   Stretched   Unsure   Energized

STRATEGIC TIP: If you circled *Curious* or *Unsure*, list one resource, an article, a mentor, a short video, you'll explore to help you move toward clarity.

Puzzle Piece	Fillable Statement
	I felt
	today because
	Before deciding what's next, I may need to
	(read, watch, ask, or reflect) to gain clarity.
	If you already know the next step, add:
	When I have that clarity, tomorrow I will

WHY IT MATTERS

Great strategic thinkers **notice weak signals before they become headlines**. Today's practice sharpens your ability to connect external trends to your organization's long-term strategy, so you can anticipate and adapt rather than simply react.

Day 10 — Horizon Scanning

Practice linking what you learn from the outside world to the decisions you make inside your organization.

MORNING PROMPT (~5 MIN)

Pause and write:

"Which external development, technology, policy, market trend, or cultural shift, could create both an opportunity and a risk for us within the next 12–36 months?"

List one or two examples and briefly describe why each could be both helpful and disruptive.

SCAN THE HORIZON (~5–10 MIN)

Find **one article, podcast, or short video** beyond your usual sources, for example:

- an international economic outlook,
- a breakthrough in clean energy,
- a cultural or demographic trend.

Note in a sentence or two: **What potential double-edged impact (opportunity and risk) might this signal for our strategy?**

ASK A STRATEGIC QUESTION (~5 MIN)

Choose a current initiative and ask:

"If this trend turns out to be more disruptive than we expect, what must we do now to stay ahead?"

Capture your first thoughts, don't worry about being precise; this is about exercising strategic foresight.

Whenever you face a meaningful decision, pause briefly:

"Does this choice move us closer to where we want to be in 1–3 years?"

Record a quick yes/no or a few words to capture your reasoning.

END-OF-DAY CHECK

Circle the word that best reflects your mindset tonight:

Clear   **Curious**   **Stretched**   **Unsure**   **Energized**

STRATEGIC TIP: If you circled *Curious* or *Unsure*, list one resource, an article, a mentor, a short video, you'll explore to help you move toward clarity.

Puzzle Piece	Fillable Statement
	I felt
	today because
	Before deciding what's next, I may need to
	(read, watch, ask, or reflect) to gain clarity.
	If you already know the next step, add:
	When I have that clarity, tomorrow I will

WHY IT MATTERS

Strategic thinkers recognize that **every external change carries both promise and risk**. By exploring both sides of emerging trends, you develop the discipline to prepare, not just react, when opportunities and challenges arrive together.

Day 11 – Horizon Scanning

GOAL

Sharpen your ability to connect external signals to the strategic choices you're making right now.

MORNING PROMPT (~5 MIN)

Pause and write:

"What change or trend I've noticed this week, inside or outside my industry, deserves a deeper look before we make our next big decision?"

Name one trend or event and briefly describe why it matters.

....

....

SCAN THE HORIZON (~5–10 MIN)

Find one source well outside your everyday reading, for example:

- a breakthrough in artificial intelligence,
- a shift in global demographics,
- a new public-policy proposal.

Jot a sentence or two: How could this development influence the way we allocate resources or set priorities over the next 12–36 months?

....

....

ASK A STRATEGIC QUESTION (~5 MIN)

Pick a current initiative and ask:

"If this trend accelerates or takes an unexpected turn, what would we need to change in our plan?"

Capture your first thoughts, this is about exercising foresight, not predicting perfectly.

....

....

Whenever you face a meaningful decision, pause briefly:

"Does this choice move us closer to where we want to be in 1–3 years?"

Record a quick yes/no or a few words explaining your reasoning.

END-OF-DAY CHECK

Circle the word that best describes your mindset tonight:

Clear   **Curious**   **Stretched**   **Unsure**   **Energized**

STRATEGIC TIP: If you circled *Curious* or *Unsure*, list one resource, an article, a mentor, a short video, you'll explore to help you move toward clarity.

Puzzle Piece	Fillable Statement
	I felt
	today because
	Before deciding what's next, I may need to
	(read, watch, ask, or reflect) to gain clarity.
	If you already know the next step, add:
	When I have that clarity, tomorrow I will

WHY IT MATTERS

Strategic thinkers know that **early signals rarely announce themselves with certainty**. Pausing to notice what deserves deeper study helps you anticipate the implications of emerging trends and make choices that stand the test of time.

Day 12 — Horizon Scanning

Practice noticing subtle "weak signals" and translating them into strategic insight.

MORNING PROMPT (~5 MIN)

Pause and write:

"What small shift I've observed this week, inside my organization or in the wider world, might be the early sign of something bigger?"

Capture even small hints: a customer comment, a policy rumor, a quiet trend in technology or culture.

SCAN THE HORIZON (~5–10 MIN)

Choose one piece of content beyond your usual field, for example:

- a scientific discovery,
- a social-behavior trend,
- an emerging economic indicator.

Jot a brief note: What possible long-term opportunity or risk does this signal?

ASK A STRATEGIC QUESTION (~5 MIN)

Select a current project or decision and ask:

"If this weak signal grows stronger over the next year, what would we need to start preparing for today?"

Write your first thoughts without editing, this is about exploration, not certainty.

Whenever a meaningful decision arises, pause briefly:

"Does this choice move us closer to where we want to be in 1–3 years?"

Record a quick yes/no or a few words explaining your reasoning.

END-OF-DAY CHECK

Circle the word that best captures your mindset tonight:

Clear   Curious   Stretched   Unsure   Energized

STRATEGIC TIP: If you circled *Curious* or *Unsure*, list one resource, an article, a mentor, a short video, you'll explore to help you move toward clarity.

Puzzle Piece	Fillable Statement
	I felt
	today because
	Before deciding what's next, I may need to
	(read, watch, ask, or reflect) to gain clarity.
	If you already know the next step, add:
	When I have that clarity, tomorrow I will

WHY IT MATTERS

Strategic thinkers excel at spotting **weak signals**, the subtle indicators that bigger changes are on the horizon. Today's practice helps you detect early cues and connect them to long-term strategy before competitors even notice.

Day 13 — Horizon Scanning

GOAL

Strengthen your ability to link faint external signals to meaningful long-term strategy.

MORNING PROMPT   (~5 MIN)

Pause and write your response to this question:

"What new idea, shift, or conversation I've encountered this week might reshape our priorities in the next 1–3 years?"

Even if it feels small or uncertain, name it and briefly describe why it caught your attention.

SCAN THE HORIZON   (~5–10 MIN)

Find one source outside your regular reading, for example:

- a global health or climate update,
- a breakthrough in artificial intelligence,
- a new social or demographic trend.

Write a quick note: *How could this development influence our organization's long-term strategy or the way we make decisions?*

ASK A STRATEGIC QUESTION   (~5 MIN)

Choose a current project or issue and ask:

"If this emerging signal proves significant, what early moves should we consider to position ourselves ahead of the curve?"

Capture your first thoughts, don't worry about being precise; the aim is to exercise foresight.

When a meaningful decision comes up, pause briefly:

"Does this action keep us aligned with where we want to be in 1–3 years?"

Record a quick yes/no or a few words explaining your reasoning.

END-OF-DAY CHECK

Circle the word that best reflects your mindset tonight:

Clear   Curious   Stretched   Unsure   Energized

STRATEGIC TIP: If you circled *Curious* or *Unsure*, list one resource, an article, a mentor, a short video, you'll explore to help you move toward clarity.

Puzzle Piece	Fillable Statement
	I felt
	today because
	Before deciding what's next, I may need to
	(read, watch, ask, or reflect) to gain clarity.
	If you already know the next step, add:
	When I have that clarity, tomorrow I will

WHY IT MATTERS

Strategic thinkers look for **patterns in small signals** and translate them into proactive action. Today's practice builds the discipline to connect what you notice today to the decisions that will matter tomorrow.

Day 14 — Horizon Scanning

Pause to gather the insights you've collected all week and decide how they might inform your next strategic moves.

MORNING PROMPT (~5 MIN)

Pause and write:

"Which external signal or trend I noticed this week has the greatest potential to shape our success in the next 1–3 years, and why?"

List one or two signals and capture why they stand out.

SCAN THE HORIZON (~5–10 MIN)

Select **one more source beyond your normal field**, it could be:

- a global economic update,
- a breakthrough in sustainability,
- a shift in consumer or workforce behavior.

Jot a brief note: What possibility or risk does this signal for our organization's long-term strategy?

ASK A STRATEGIC QUESTION (~5 MIN)

Choose a current initiative and ask:

"If this signal accelerates or becomes the new norm, what early actions would give us an advantage?"

Write your first thoughts, this is about practicing foresight, not predicting perfectly.

Whenever you face a meaningful decision, pause briefly:

"Does this action keep us aligned with where we want to be in 1–3 years?"

Record a quick yes/no or a few words capturing your reasoning.

....

END-OF-DAY CHECK

Circle the word that best matches your mindset tonight:

Clear   **Curious**   **Stretched**   **Unsure**   **Energized**

STRATEGIC TIP: If you circled *Curious* or *Unsure*, list one resource, an article, a mentor, a short video, you'll explore to help you move toward clarity.

....

Puzzle Piece	Fillable Statement
	I felt _______________
	today because _______________
	Before deciding what's next, I may need to _______________
	(read, watch, ask, or reflect) to gain clarity.
	If you already know the next step, add:
	When I have that clarity, tomorrow I will _______________

WHY IT MATTERS

Strategic thinkers pause to connect the dots across multiple signals. Today's reflection turns a week of scanning into actionable insight so external trends become catalysts for deliberate strategy, not just interesting news.

Week 2 Strategic Challenge – Horizon Scanning

SCENARIO:

A breakthrough technology emerges in an unrelated industry.

It's too early to know if it will disrupt your field, but a few competitors are quietly exploring partnerships.

YOUR TASK:

1. List three clarifying questions you would ask to gauge the potential impact on your organization.

2. Identify one immediate low-risk action you could take (for example: research partnership models, schedule an expert briefing, or monitor key indicators).

3. Note the single biggest risk of doing nothing for the next year.

REFLECT:

- What does this exercise reveal about your organization's ability to respond early to weak signals?
- How might you embed horizon scanning into your regular leadership routines?

Explore additional scenarios and companion resources designed to deepen your use of **the ThinkSuite™ Strategic Intelligence Decks™**. *Visit www.pamelajgreen.com/store for details.*

Weekly Strategic Anchor

A Rhythm That Protects Your Progress

Strategic thinking isn't sustained by motivation, it's sustained by rhythm. Your Weekly Strategic Anchor is the one consistent ritual that keeps your goals, your focus, and your decisions aligned throughout the 66-day journey.

PURPOSE OF THE WEEKLY STRATEGIC ANCHOR

- Reconnect to your strategic priorities
- Review progress without judgment
- Anticipate obstacles before they derail you
- Recommit to the habits that matter most
- Make small adjustments that protect your long-term goals

Your anchor ensures you never drift too far from your intentions, even during busy or overwhelming weeks.

YOUR WEEKLY STRATEGIC ANCHOR RITUAL

Complete this every week on the same day, at the same time. Choose a moment that feels calm, available, and repeatable.

My Weekly Strategic Anchor Day & Time:

....

1. Strategic Wins This Week

What moved forward? What worked? List 2–3 wins, no matter how small.

....

....

2. What's Stuck or Slipping?

Identify challenges without blame. Awareness is your strategic leverage.

....

....

3. What Truly Mattered Most This Week?

Reflect on where your time, energy, and attention actually went.

....

....

4. One Strategic Action for the Next 24 Hours

Choose the smallest meaningful action that moves your priority forward.

My One Action:
....

....

....

5. What Support or Resources Do I Need?

Strategic thinkers don't do it alone.

....

....

....

6. Alignment Check

Are my actions aligned with my long-term goals and values?

☐ Yes, keep going

☐ Not fully, what adjustment do I need to make?

Adjustment Needed (if any):

....

....

STRATEGIC INTEGRATION

"What does the strategic version of me need next week?"
Write your answer in one clear sentence:

....

....

....

Chance favors
the prepared
mind.
- LOUIS PASTEUR

Day 15 — Strategic Questions

Begin the week by using powerful questions to stretch your thinking and uncover hidden opportunities.

MORNING PROMPT (~5 MIN)

Pause and write:

"What big decision or challenge am I facing right now that would benefit from a powerful question rather than a quick answer?"

List the decision or challenge and the first question that comes to mind.

SCAN THE HORIZON (~5–10 MIN)

Select and read, listen to, or watch one brief source outside your usual field, perhaps:

- a leadership case study,
- an innovation article,
- a cultural or demographic trend piece.

Jot a sentence or two: What new question does this spark about our strategy or future?

ASK A STRATEGIC QUESTION (~5 MIN)

Choose a current initiative and ask one of these, or craft your own:

- "What would success look like in three years?"
- "What risk are we not talking about?"
- "What hidden opportunity could this challenge reveal?"

Capture your initial thoughts, don't worry about having the answer; the goal is to practice asking better questions.

Whenever a meaningful decision arises, pause briefly:

"Does this action keep us aligned with where we want to be in 1–3 years?"

Record a quick yes/no or a few words to explain your reasoning.

END-OF-DAY CHECK

Circle the word that best matches your mindset tonight:

Clear   Curious   Stretched   Unsure   Energized

STRATEGIC TIP: If you circled *Curious* or *Unsure*, list one resource, an article, a mentor, a short video, you'll explore to help you move toward clarity.

Puzzle Piece	Fillable Statement
	I felt ....
	today because ....
	....
	Before deciding what's next, I may need to ....
	....
	(read, watch, ask, or reflect) to gain clarity.
	If you already know the next step, add:
	When I have that clarity, tomorrow I will ....
	....

WHY IT MATTERS

Strategic thinkers know that the quality of their questions determines the quality of their insights. By deliberately framing and refining powerful questions, you create space for better options and stronger long-term decisions.

Day 16 — Strategic Questions

Use intentional questions to see beyond the obvious and challenge your default assumptions.

MORNING PROMPT   (~5 MIN)

Pause and write:

"Which assumption I'm holding about a project, decision, or relationship might deserve to be questioned today?"

Name the assumption and, if you can, why it might need a closer look.

....

....

SCAN THE HORIZON   (~5–10 MIN)

Find one short article, podcast, or video outside your usual field, for example:

- a breakthrough in health or science,
- a social or cultural shift,
- a global economic development.

Jot a brief note: *What question does this new information raise about our strategy or my own leadership choices?*

....

....

ASK A STRATEGIC QUESTION   (~5 MIN)

Pick a current initiative and ask:

"If our key assumption here proves wrong, what would we need to change, immediately and over the next year?"

Write your first thoughts, no need to be precise; the goal is to practice challenging your own thinking.

....

....

Whenever a meaningful decision arises, pause briefly:

"Does this action keep us aligned with where we want to be in 1–3 years?"

Record a quick yes/no or a few words explaining your reasoning.

END-OF-DAY CHECK

Circle the word that best captures your mindset tonight:

Clear   **Curious**   **Stretched**   **Unsure**   **Energized**

STRATEGIC TIP: If you circled *Curious* or *Unsure*, list one resource, an article, a mentor, a short video, you'll explore to help you move toward clarity.

Puzzle Piece	Fillable Statement
	I felt
	today because
	Before deciding what's next, I may need to
	(read, watch, ask, or reflect) to gain clarity.
	If you already know the next step, add:
	When I have that clarity, tomorrow I will

WHY IT MATTERS

Strategic thinkers excel at surfacing and testing hidden assumptions. By deliberately questioning what you "know," you reduce blind spots and open space for innovative solutions and a stronger long-term strategy.

Day 17 — Strategic Questions

Strengthen your ability to use powerful questions to uncover hidden opportunities and risks.

MORNING PROMPT   **(~5 MIN)**

Pause and write:

"What decision or issue on my plate right now might benefit from a completely different perspective?"

Name the decision or issue and briefly describe why a fresh perspective could reveal something new.

....

....

SCAN THE HORIZON   **(~5–10 MIN)**

Choose one short article, podcast, or video outside your usual field, for example:

- a breakthrough in digital technology,
- an emerging demographic trend,
- a shift in public policy.

Jot a sentence or two: What unexpected question does this raise about our long-term strategy or about how we lead today?

....

....

ASK A STRATEGIC QUESTION   **(~5 MIN)**

Pick a current project or challenge and ask:

"If someone with no stake in this decision were advising us, what question would they ask first?"

Capture the first thoughts that come to you. The goal is to see the situation from a viewpoint you might normally miss.

....

....

Whenever you face a meaningful decision, pause briefly:

"Does this action move us closer to where we want to be in 1–3 years?"

Record a quick yes/no or a few words capturing your reasoning.

END-OF-DAY CHECK

Circle the word that best matches your mindset tonight:

Clear   **Curious**   **Stretched**   **Unsure**   **Energized**

STRATEGIC TIP: If you circled *Curious* or *Unsure*, list one resource, an article, a mentor, a short video, you'll explore to help you move toward clarity.

Puzzle Piece	Fillable Statement
	I felt
	today because
	Before deciding what's next, I may need to
	(read, watch, ask, or reflect) to gain clarity.
	If you already know the next step, add:
	When I have that clarity, tomorrow I will

WHY IT MATTERS

Strategic thinkers actively seek perspectives beyond their own. Inviting an "outsider's question" helps you break out of habitual thinking and spot opportunities or risks you might otherwise overlook.

Day 18 — Strategic Questions

Practice asking deeper questions that reveal what truly drives long-term success.

MORNING PROMPT (~5 MIN)

Pause and write:

"What outcome do I most want to protect or achieve over the next 1–3 years, and what question will help me test whether today's work supports it?"

Identify the outcome and draft the question you'll use to keep yourself (and others) focused on it today.

SCAN THE HORIZON (~5–10 MIN)

Find one article, podcast, or video outside your normal field, perhaps:

- a new economic forecast,
- a breakthrough in science or technology,
- a piece on changing social or workforce expectations.

Note in a sentence or two: *What question does this raise about our strategy or the assumptions we're making?*

ASK A STRATEGIC QUESTION (~5 MIN)

Choose a current initiative and ask:

"If our most important long-term goal suddenly became much harder to reach, what would we need to rethink right now?"

Capture your first thoughts, don't aim for perfect answers; focus on stretching your perspective.

Whenever a meaningful decision arises, pause briefly:

"Does this action move us closer to where we want to be in 1–3 years?"

Record a quick yes/no or a few words explaining your reasoning.

END-OF-DAY CHECK

Circle the word that best describes your mindset tonight:

Clear   **Curious**   **Stretched**   **Unsure**   **Energized**

STRATEGIC TIP: If you circled *Curious* or *Unsure*, list one resource, an article, a mentor, a short video, you'll explore to help you move toward clarity.

Puzzle Piece	Fillable Statement
	I felt
	today because
	Before deciding what's next, I may need to
	(read, watch, ask, or reflect) to gain clarity.
	If you already know the next step, add:
	When I have that clarity, tomorrow I will

WHY IT MATTERS

Strategic thinkers keep their **long-term outcomes visible even when daily pressures compete for attention**. By naming the results you most want to protect and framing questions that test every decision against those results, you strengthen both focus and foresight.

Day 19 — Strategic Questions

Use probing questions to uncover hidden risks and opportunities before they surface.

MORNING PROMPT (~5 MIN)

Pause and write:

"What is one risk, internal or external, that we might be underestimating right now, and what question can help bring it into the open?"

Name the risk (even if it's only a hunch) and the question you'll use to explore it.

SCAN THE HORIZON (~5–10 MIN)

Choose **one article, podcast, or short video outside your usual field**, for example:

- a global economic outlook,
- a breakthrough in medical or environmental science,
- a demographic or cultural trend.

Jot a brief note: What risk or hidden opportunity does this information suggest for our organization's next 1–3 years?

ASK A STRATEGIC QUESTION (~5 MIN)

Select a current initiative or decision and ask:

"If this risk materializes sooner than expected, how would we need to adapt our strategy?"

Write your initial thoughts; don't worry about being definitive; the goal is to build the habit of proactive questioning.

When a meaningful decision arises, pause briefly:

"Does this action move us closer to where we want to be in 1–3 years?"

Record a quick yes/no or a few words explaining your reasoning.

END-OF-DAY CHECK

Circle the word that best captures your mindset tonight:

Clear   **Curious**   **Stretched**   **Unsure**   **Energized**

STRATEGIC TIP: If you circled *Curious* or *Unsure*, list one resource, an article, a mentor, a short video, you'll explore to help you move toward clarity.

Puzzle Piece	Fillable Statement
	I felt
	today because
	Before deciding what's next, I may need to
	(read, watch, ask, or reflect) to gain clarity.
	If you already know the next step, add:
	When I have that clarity, tomorrow I will

WHY IT MATTERS

Strategic thinkers **surface risks early**, not to predict every outcome, but to reduce surprises and create options. Today's practice strengthens your ability to spot what might go wrong and to ask the questions that transform potential threats into informed strategy.

Day 20 — Strategic Questions

Strengthen the discipline of asking questions that reveal possibilities others may overlook.

MORNING PROMPT   (~5 MIN)

Pause and write:

"What opportunity might be hiding in plain sight, inside or outside our organization, and what question will help me uncover it today?"

Identify the opportunity you suspect and the key question that could bring it into focus.

SCAN THE HORIZON   (~5–10 MIN)

Find one article, podcast, or video beyond your usual field, for example:

- a new technology breakthrough,
- a shift in consumer preferences,
- a policy or regulatory change.

Write a quick note: *What question does this raise about how we create or capture value in the next 1–3 years?*

ASK A STRATEGIC QUESTION   (~5 MIN)

Choose a current initiative and ask:

"If we approached this challenge from the perspective of a competitor or an outsider, what opportunity would they see that we don't?"

Capture your first thoughts, don't aim for certainty; focus on widening your lens.

Whenever a meaningful decision arises, pause briefly:

"Does this action move us closer to where we want to be in 1–3 years?"

Record a quick yes/no or a few words explaining your reasoning.

END-OF-DAY CHECK

Circle the word that best describes your mindset tonight:

Clear   Curious   Stretched   Unsure   Energized

STRATEGIC TIP: If you circled *Curious* or *Unsure*, list one resource, an article, a mentor, a short video, you'll explore to help you move toward clarity.

Puzzle Piece	Fillable Statement
	I felt
	today because
	Before deciding what's next, I may need to
	(read, watch, ask, or reflect) to gain clarity.
	If you already know the next step, add:
	When I have that clarity, tomorrow I will

WHY IT MATTERS

Strategic thinkers look beyond obvious answers to discover **hidden opportunities**. By asking questions that challenge assumptions and invite fresh viewpoints, you sharpen your ability to spot possibilities before others even notice them.

Day 21 — Strategic Questions

Pull together the insights from a week of powerful questioning and notice how your thinking has shifted.

MORNING PROMPT (~5 MIN)

Pause and write:

"Looking back over this week, which strategic question sparked the biggest insight for me, and why?"

Capture the question and the key realization it led to.

....

....

SCAN THE HORIZON (~5–10 MIN)

Choose **one article, podcast, or short video outside your usual field**, for example:

- a breakthrough in energy or climate science,
- a social or cultural trend,
- an unexpected innovation in another industry.

Jot a sentence or two: *What fresh question does this raise about our long-term strategy?*

....

....

ASK A STRATEGIC QUESTION (~5 MIN)

Select a current initiative and ask:

"If we suddenly had to double the impact of this work in the next year, what would need to change today?"

Write your first thoughts, don't aim for perfect answers; the goal is to keep stretching your strategic perspective.

....

....

Whenever a meaningful decision arises, pause briefly:

"Does this action move us closer to where we want to be in 1–3 years?"

Record a quick yes/no or a few words explaining your reasoning.

END-OF-DAY CHECK

Circle the word that best matches your mindset tonight:

Clear   Curious   Stretched   Unsure   Energized

STRATEGIC TIP: If you circled *Curious* or *Unsure*, list one resource, an article, a mentor, a short video, you'll explore to help you move toward clarity.

Puzzle Piece	Fillable Statement
	I felt
	today because
	Before deciding what's next, I may need to
	(read, watch, ask, or reflect) to gain clarity.
	If you already know the next step, add:
	When I have that clarity, tomorrow I will

WHY IT MATTERS

Strategic thinkers know that **breakthroughs often begin with the right question, not the right answer**. Pausing to identify the questions that generated your best insights this week reinforces the habit of inquiry that drives long-term success.

Week 3 Strategic Challenge – Strategic Questions

SCENARIO:

Your leadership team is planning next year's budget. Several departments are lobbying for additional funding, but you suspect the organization hasn't asked the deeper questions needed to set true strategic priorities.

YOUR TASK:

1. Write three powerful questions you would pose to the team before any funding decisions are made.

2. Identify one question that could surface hidden risks or overlooked opportunities.

3. Describe how asking these questions might shift the conversation or the eventual budget choices.

REFLECT:

- What does this exercise reveal about how you typically prepare for high-stakes decisions?
- How might you integrate strategic questioning into your regular leadership practices?

To continue sharpening your strategic thinking, explore additional scenarios in the **ThinkSuite™ Strategic Intelligence Decks™**, *visit www.pamelajgreen.com/store for details.*

Weekly Strategic Anchor

A Rhythm That Protects Your Progress

Strategic thinking isn't sustained by motivation, it's sustained by rhythm.

Your Weekly Strategic Anchor is the one consistent ritual that keeps your goals, your focus, and your decisions aligned throughout the 66-day journey.

PURPOSE OF THE WEEKLY STRATEGIC ANCHOR

- Reconnect to your strategic priorities
- Review progress without judgment
- Anticipate obstacles before they derail you
- Recommit to the habits that matter most
- Make small adjustments that protect your long-term goals

Your anchor ensures you never drift too far from your intentions, even during busy or overwhelming weeks.

YOUR WEEKLY STRATEGIC ANCHOR RITUAL

Complete this every week on the same day, at the same time. Choose a moment that feels calm, available, and repeatable.

My Weekly Strategic Anchor Day & Time:

....

1. Strategic Wins This Week

What moved forward? What worked? List 2–3 wins, no matter how small.

....

....

2. What's Stuck or Slipping?

Identify challenges without blame. Awareness is your strategic leverage.

....

....

3. What Truly Mattered Most This Week?

Reflect on where your time, energy, and attention actually went.
The Three Priorities That Mattered Most:

1. ....

2. ....

3. ....

4. One Strategic Action for the Next 24 Hours

Choose the smallest meaningful action that moves your priority forward.

My One Action:

5. What Support or Resources Do I Need?

Strategic thinkers don't do it alone.

6. Alignment Check

Are my actions aligned with my long-term goals and values?

☐ Yes, keep going

☐ Not fully, what adjustment do I need to make?

Adjustment Needed (if any):

STRATEGIC INTEGRATION

"What does the strategic version of me need next week?"
Write your answer in one clear sentence:

Phase 2 — Application (Days 22–42)

With your strategic muscles warmed up, it's time to put them to work in real decisions. In this phase we move from awareness to **applied strategy**:

Alignment Check	**Systems Thinking**	**Trade-Off Discipline**
Testing whether your daily choices reinforce your long-term vision.	Seeing your organization as a living network where every move creates ripple effects.	Naming both the gains and the sacrifices behind every "yes."

This is where strategic thinking gets real, and sometimes uncomfortable. You'll discover that clarity comes as much from what you choose **not** to do as from what you pursue. These three weeks will stretch you to balance competing priorities and to communicate tough choices with confidence.

Leadership is not
a destination—
it's a journey
that requires an
open mind and
a willingness to
learn.

- URSUAL BURNS

Day 22 — Alignment Check

GOAL

Begin exploring how well your daily choices align with your organization's long-term strategy and desired outcomes.

MORNING PROMPT　　　　　　　　　　　　　(~5 MIN)

Pause and write:

"Which decision or action on my agenda today most needs to be tested for strategic alignment?"

Name the decision or action and briefly describe why it could affect long-term goals.

SCAN THE HORIZON　　　　　　　　　　(~5–10 MIN)

Select and read, listen to, or watch one article, podcast, or short video outside your normal field, for example:

- a case study of a company that lost focus,
- a policy change that could alter your industry,
- a story of an organization realigning its strategy.

Jot a quick note: *What insight or caution does this give me about staying aligned with our 1–3 year strategy?*

ASK A STRATEGIC QUESTION　　　　　　　(~5 MIN)

Choose a current project or initiative and ask:

"If our long-term strategy is the destination, how does this decision move us closer, or take us off course?"

Capture your first thoughts. The aim is to strengthen the habit of testing alignment before acting.

Whenever you face a meaningful decision, pause briefly:

"Does this action keep us aligned with where we want to be in 1–3 years?"

Record a quick yes/no or a few words capturing your reasoning.

END-OF-DAY CHECK

Circle the word that best matches your mindset tonight:

Clear   **Curious**   **Stretched**   **Unsure**   **Energized**

STRATEGIC TIP: If you circled *Curious* or *Unsure*, list one resource, an article, a mentor, a short video, you'll explore to help you move toward clarity.

Puzzle Piece	Fillable Statement
	I felt
	today because
	Before deciding what's next, I may need to
	(read, watch, ask, or reflect) to gain clarity.
	If you already know the next step, add:
	When I have that clarity, tomorrow I will

WHY IT MATTERS

Strategic thinkers know that **alignment is what turns strategy into results**. By making a habit of checking whether each decision supports your long-term goals, you help your organization stay focused and avoid the drift that undermines impact.

Day 23 — Alignment Check

GOAL

Build the habit of testing every key decision against the organization's long-term strategy.

MORNING PROMPT (~5 MIN)

Pause and write:

"What meeting, project, or decision today could easily drift away from our 1–3 year strategy if I'm not careful?"

Name it and briefly note why it could slide off course.

SCAN THE HORIZON (~5–10 MIN)

Read, watch, or listen to one short piece outside your usual field, for example:

- a case study of a company that pivoted too quickly,
- an article on regulatory or economic changes,
- a story about how a mission-driven organization maintained focus.

Jot a sentence or two: What lesson or caution does this give me about keeping our actions aligned with our strategic destination?

ASK A STRATEGIC QUESTION (~5 MIN)

Pick a current initiative and ask:

"If this decision takes us off course, what early warning sign would I notice first?"

Capture your first thoughts, don't worry about being exact; the aim is to strengthen your instinct for spotting misalignment early.

When a meaningful decision comes up, pause briefly:

"Does this action move us closer to where we want to be in 1–3 years?"

Record a quick yes/no or a few words explaining your reasoning.

END-OF-DAY CHECK

Circle the word that best describes your mindset tonight:

Clear   **Curious**   **Stretched**   **Unsure**   **Energized**

STRATEGIC TIP: If you circled *Curious* or *Unsure*, list one resource, an article, a mentor, a short video, you'll explore to help you move toward clarity.

Puzzle Piece	Fillable Statement
	I felt
	today because
	Before deciding what's next, I may need to
	(read, watch, ask, or reflect) to gain clarity.
	If you already know the next step, add:
	When I have that clarity, tomorrow I will

WHY IT MATTERS

Strategic thinkers stay alert to **drift**, the slow, subtle pull away from long-term goals.

Today's practice helps you recognize early signs of misalignment and make small course corrections before they become costly detours.

Day 24 — Alignment Check

Deepen your ability to connect daily activity to long-term strategic goals and spot when work begins to drift.

MORNING PROMPT   (~5 MIN)

Pause and write:

"Which of today's tasks or decisions could create a gap between what we say is important and what we actually do?"

Name the task or decision and briefly explain the possible gap.

SCAN THE HORIZON   (~5–10 MIN)

Choose one article, podcast, or short video outside your usual field, for example:

- a story about a company that lost focus chasing short-term gains,
- an update on shifting market or policy priorities,
- an analysis of how an organization successfully re-aligned its strategy.

Jot a quick note: What lesson does this example offer about keeping our actions and strategy in sync?

ASK A STRATEGIC QUESTION   (~5 MIN)

Select a current project or initiative and ask:

"If someone looked only at how we spend our time and resources, would they clearly see our long-term strategy?"

Capture your first thoughts, this question helps you test whether actions match intentions.

When a meaningful decision arises, pause briefly:

"Does this action move us closer to where we want to be in 1–3 years?"

Record a quick yes/no or a few words to capture your reasoning.

END-OF-DAY CHECK

Circle the word that best captures your mindset tonight:

Clear   Curious   Stretched   Unsure   Energized

STRATEGIC TIP: If you circled *Curious* or *Unsure*, list one resource, an article, a mentor, a short video, you'll explore to help you move toward clarity.

Puzzle Piece	Fillable Statement
	I felt
	today because
	Before deciding what's next, I may need to
	(read, watch, ask, or reflect) to gain clarity.
	If you already know the next step, add:
	When I have that clarity, tomorrow I will

WHY IT MATTERS

Strategic thinking isn't only about setting big goals, it's about ensuring **daily behaviors reinforce those goals**. Today's practice helps you notice when your organization's stated priorities and its actual actions begin to diverge, so you can close the gap early.

Day 25 — Alignment Check

GOAL

Strengthen your instinct to pause and verify that today's choices truly support long-term strategy.

MORNING PROMPT   (~5 MIN)

Pause and write:

"What decision or activity today could appear productive in the short term but might weaken our long-term strategy if left unchecked?"

Name it and briefly explain the potential trade-off.

....

....

SCAN THE HORIZON   (~5–10 MIN)

Select and read, listen to, or watch one article, **podcast, or short video outside your usual field**, for example:

- a case study of a company that sacrificed long-term success for quick wins,
- a policy or regulatory change with long-term implications,
- a story about an organization that course-corrected to realign with its mission.

Jot a sentence or two: What caution or insight does this give me about maintaining strategic alignment?

....

....

ASK A STRATEGIC QUESTION   (~5 MIN)

Choose a current project or decision and ask:

"If we look back in three years, how will this decision prove that we stayed true to our strategy?"

Capture your first thoughts, don't worry about being precise; the goal is to test alignment before acting.

....

....

Whenever you face a meaningful decision, pause briefly:

"Does this action move us closer to where we want to be in 1–3 years?"

Record a quick yes/no or a few words to capture your reasoning.

END-OF-DAY CHECK

Circle the word that best describes your mindset tonight:

Clear   Curious   Stretched   Unsure   Energized

STRATEGIC TIP: If you circled *Curious* or *Unsure*, list one resource, an article, a mentor, a short video, you'll explore to help you move toward clarity.

Puzzle Piece	Fillable Statement
	I felt
	today because
	Before deciding what's next, I may need to
	(read, watch, ask, or reflect) to gain clarity.
	If you already know the next step, add:
	When I have that clarity, tomorrow I will

WHY IT MATTERS

Strategic alignment can be undermined by **short-term wins that distract from the bigger goal**.

Today's practice trains you to spot those tempting detours early so you can protect the long-term vision.

Day 26 – Alignment Check

Reinforce the habit of checking that daily actions, and the way you communicate them, stay true to your long-term strategy.

MORNING PROMPT (~5 MIN)

Pause and write:

"What message, update, or decision I share today needs to clearly reflect our long-term strategy?"

Identify the message or decision and briefly note why it's important that others see its strategic connection.

SCAN THE HORIZON (~5–10 MIN)

Choose **one article, podcast, or short video outside your usual field**, such as:

- a story of a company that successfully realigned its messaging with its mission,
- a case of an organization losing credibility by sending mixed signals,
- an analysis of how clear communication reinforced strategic goals.

Jot a sentence or two: *What lesson does this example offer about communicating alignment?*

ASK A STRATEGIC QUESTION (~5 MIN)

Select a current initiative and ask:

"If someone unfamiliar with our strategy heard today's message or watched our actions, would they see how it connects to our long-term goals?"

Capture your first thoughts, this question helps ensure your communication and decisions both reflect strategic intent.

Whenever you face a meaningful decision, pause briefly:

"Does this action move us closer to where we want to be in 1–3 years?"

Record a quick yes/no or a few words explaining your reasoning.

END-OF-DAY CHECK

Circle the word that best captures your mindset tonight:

Clear   Curious   Stretched   Unsure   Energized

STRATEGIC TIP: If you circled *Curious* or *Unsure*, list one resource, an article, a mentor, a short video, you'll explore to help you move toward clarity.

Puzzle Piece	Fillable Statement
	I felt
	today because
	Before deciding what's next, I may need to
	(read, watch, ask, or reflect) to gain clarity.
	If you already know the next step, add:
	When I have that clarity, tomorrow I will

WHY IT MATTERS

Strategic alignment isn't only about **what decisions you make, it's also about how you communicate them**. Today's practice reinforces the discipline of making sure your words and actions consistently signal the organization's long-term direction.

Day 27 — Alignment Check

GOAL

Strengthen your ability to notice when short-term pressures could pull your team away from long-term priorities.

MORNING PROMPT   (~5 MIN)

Pause and write:

"Where am I feeling the greatest pressure to deliver quick results, and how might that pressure tempt us to drift from our 1–3 year strategy?"

Name the pressure point and briefly describe the risk it creates.

SCAN THE HORIZON   (~5–10 MIN)

Read, watch, or listen to **one piece outside your normal field**, for example:

- a story about a company that sacrificed long-term goals for short-term gains,
- an article on how organizations balance quarterly results with long-range vision,
- a policy change that forces immediate action but may conflict with strategic plans.

Jot a sentence or two: *What insight or caution does this give me about holding the long view under pressure?*

ASK A STRATEGIC QUESTION   (~5 MIN)

Select a current project or decision and ask:

"If we choose speed over strategy here, what might we regret a year from now?"

Write your first thoughts, don't worry about being precise; the goal is to surface possible trade-offs.

When a meaningful decision arises, pause briefly:

"Does this action move us closer to where we want to be in 1–3 years?"

Record a quick yes/no or a few words to capture your reasoning.

END-OF-DAY CHECK

Circle the word that best describes your mindset tonight:

Clear   Curious   Stretched   Unsure   Energized

STRATEGIC TIP: If you circled *Curious* or *Unsure*, list one resource, an article, a mentor, a short video, you'll explore to help you move toward clarity.

Puzzle Piece	Fillable Statement
	I felt
	today because
	Before deciding what's next, I may need to
	(read, watch, ask, or reflect) to gain clarity.
	If you already know the next step, add:
	When I have that clarity, tomorrow I will

WHY IT MATTERS

Strategic thinkers learn to **resist the pull of short-term wins when they threaten long-term goals**. Today's practice helps you recognize when urgency might override strategy so you can stay anchored to your true priorities.

Day 28 — Alignment Check

GOAL

Pause to consolidate everything you've noticed this week about how well daily actions align with long-term strategy.

MORNING PROMPT (~5 MIN)

Pause and write:

"Looking back over the past week, where did I see the strongest evidence of alignment with our 1–3 year strategy, and where did I notice the greatest risk of drift?"

List at least one example of each.

SCAN THE HORIZON (~5–10 MIN)

Select and read, listen to, or watch one short article, podcast, or video outside your usual field, such as:

- a story about a company that course-corrected to realign with its mission,
- a policy or regulatory update that forced strategic adjustments,
- an analysis of how leaders maintained focus during a disruptive period.

Jot a sentence or two: *What lesson does this offer about protecting strategic alignment under changing conditions?*

ASK A STRATEGIC QUESTION (~5 MIN)

Select a current initiative and ask:

"If we suddenly lost sight of our long-term strategy, what early warning sign would appear first, and how could we respond quickly?"

Capture your first thoughts, don't worry about precision; the aim is to identify signals of misalignment.

Whenever a meaningful decision arises, pause briefly:

"Does this action move us closer to where we want to be in 1–3 years?"

Record a quick yes/no or a few words to capture your reasoning.

END-OF-DAY CHECK

Circle the word that best matches your mindset tonight:

Clear   Curious   Stretched   Unsure   Energized

STRATEGIC TIP: If you circled *Curious* or *Unsure*, list one resource, an article, a mentor, a short video, you'll explore to help you move toward clarity.

Puzzle Piece	Fillable Statement
	I felt
	today because
	Before deciding what's next, I may need to
	(read, watch, ask, or reflect) to gain clarity.
	If you already know the next step, add:
	When I have that clarity, tomorrow I will

WHY IT MATTERS

Strategic alignment isn't a one-time event; it's a **continuous practice**. Reflecting on both the moments of strong alignment and the areas where you sensed drift helps you strengthen the habits that keep your strategy alive in daily work.

Week 4 Strategic Challenge – Alignment Check

SCENARIO:

Midway through the fiscal year, your organization faces unexpected budget pressure.

Several leaders propose cutting long-term initiatives to meet short-term targets, while others argue for protecting strategic investments.

YOUR TASK:

1. Identify the two or three **core priorities** that must be protected to stay true to the 3-year strategy.

2. Draft **three questions** you would pose to the leadership team before making any cuts.

3. Outline a **quick action plan** to communicate decisions so the organization remains confident and focused.

REFLECT:

- How do you normally balance short-term demands with long-term commitments?
- What does this reveal about your own instinct for maintaining alignment when the pressure is on?

To continue sharpening your strategic thinking, explore more scenarios in the **ThinkSuite™ Strategic Intelligence Decks™**, *visit www.pamelajgreen.com/store for details.*

Weekly Strategic Anchor

A Rhythm That Protects Your Progress

Strategic thinking isn't sustained by motivation, it's sustained by rhythm.

Your Weekly Strategic Anchor is the one consistent ritual that keeps your goals, your focus, and your decisions aligned throughout the 66-day journey.

PURPOSE OF THE WEEKLY STRATEGIC ANCHOR

- Reconnect to your strategic priorities
- Review progress without judgment
- Anticipate obstacles before they derail you
- Recommit to the habits that matter most
- Make small adjustments that protect your long-term goals

Your anchor ensures you never drift too far from your intentions, even during busy or overwhelming weeks.

YOUR WEEKLY STRATEGIC ANCHOR RITUAL

Complete this every week on the same day, at the same time. Choose a moment that feels calm, available, and repeatable.

My Weekly Strategic Anchor Day & Time:

....

1. Strategic Wins This Week

What moved forward? What worked? List 2–3 wins, no matter how small.

....

....

2. What's Stuck or Slipping?

Identify challenges without blame. Awareness is your strategic leverage.

....

....

3. What Truly Mattered Most This Week?

Reflect on where your time, energy, and attention actually went.
The Three Priorities That Mattered Most:

1.

2.

3.

4. One Strategic Action for the Next 24 Hours

Choose the smallest meaningful action that moves your priority forward.

5. What Support or Resources Do I Need?

Strategic thinkers don't do it alone.

6. Alignment Check

Are my actions aligned with my long-term goals and values?

☐ Yes, keep going

☐ Not fully, what adjustment do I need to make?

Adjustment Needed (if any):

STRATEGIC INTEGRATION

"What does the strategic version of me need next week?"
Write your answer in one clear sentence:

You cannot deliver value unless you absorb knowledge constantly.

\- INDRA NOOYI

Day 29 — Systems Thinking

Begin to see your organization as a set of interconnected parts so you can anticipate ripple effects before acting.

MORNING PROMPT   (~5 MIN)

Pause and write:

"What decision or change I'm involved in today could create ripple effects, intended or unintended, across other teams or processes?"

Name the decision or change and briefly describe where you suspect the ripples might appear.

....

....

SCAN THE HORIZON   (~5–10 MIN)

Find one short article, podcast, or video outside your usual field, for example:

- a case study of how one industry change disrupted many others,
- an analysis of supply-chain or ecosystem effects,
- a story about a technology that reshaped multiple markets.

Jot a quick note: *What insight does this give me about how interconnected systems respond to change?*

....

....

ASK A STRATEGIC QUESTION   (~5 MIN)

Choose a current project or initiative and ask:

"If we adjust this one element, what second- or third-order consequences might follow across our organization or stakeholders?"

Capture your first thoughts, don't aim for perfect answers; the goal is to practice anticipating ripple effects.

....

Whenever you face a meaningful decision, pause briefly:

"Does this action move us closer to where we want to be in 1–3 years?"

Record a quick yes/no or a few words to capture your reasoning.

END-OF-DAY CHECK

Circle the word that best reflects your mindset tonight:

Clear   Curious   Stretched   Unsure   Energized

STRATEGIC TIP: If you circled *Curious* or *Unsure*, list one resource, an article, a mentor, a short video, you'll explore to help you move toward clarity.

Puzzle Piece	Fillable Statement
	I felt
	today because
	Before deciding what's next, I may need to
	(read, watch, ask, or reflect) to gain clarity.
	If you already know the next step, add:
	When I have that clarity, tomorrow I will

WHY IT MATTERS

Strategic thinkers understand that **organizations behave like living systems**; a shift in one area inevitably affects others. Today's practice trains you to pause and consider those ripple effects so you can act with foresight rather than simply react.

Day 30 — Systems Thinking

Deepen your ability to recognize how one decision can trigger a chain of effects across your organization or network.

MORNING PROMPT (~5 MIN)

Pause and write:

"What decision, change, or trend I'm watching today could produce an unexpected chain reaction in the next 12–36 months?"

Name the decision or trend and briefly describe where the ripple effects might appear.

SCAN THE HORIZON (~5–10 MIN)

Find one article, podcast, or short video outside your usual field, for example:

- a case study showing how a single innovation disrupted multiple industries,
- a report on how policy changes affect interconnected markets,
- a story of how small shifts in one sector created wider consequences.

Jot a sentence or two: *What lesson does this example give me about how complex systems respond to change?*

ASK A STRATEGIC QUESTION (~5 MIN)

Select a current project or initiative and ask:

"If we tweak one key element of this plan, what second- or third-order effects might follow across people, processes, or partners?"

Capture your first thoughts, don't worry about being exact; the aim is to practice anticipating ripple effects.

Whenever a meaningful decision arises, pause briefly:

"Does this action move us closer to where we want to be in 1–3 years?"

Record a quick yes/no or a few words explaining your reasoning.

END-OF-DAY CHECK

Circle the word that best matches your mindset tonight:

Clear   **Curious**   **Stretched**   **Unsure**   **Energized**

STRATEGIC TIP: If you circled *Curious* or *Unsure*, list one resource, an article, a mentor, a short video, you'll explore to help you move toward clarity.

Puzzle Piece	Fillable Statement
	I felt __________
	today because __________
	Before deciding what's next, I may need to __________
	(read, watch, ask, or reflect) to gain clarity.
	If you already know the next step, add:
	When I have that clarity, tomorrow I will __________

WHY IT MATTERS

Strategic thinkers recognize that small moves in one part of a system can create large effects elsewhere. Today's practice sharpens your ability to anticipate those hidden connections and plan for both intended and unintended consequences.

Day 31 — Systems Thinking

Build the habit of spotting relationships and dependencies so you can anticipate how change in one area impacts the whole.

MORNING PROMPT   (~5 MIN)

Pause and write:

"What process, relationship, or resource today depends on several moving parts, and what could happen if one part fails or changes unexpectedly?"

Name the process or relationship and briefly describe the possible chain reaction.

SCAN THE HORIZON   (~5–10 MIN)

Choose one article, podcast, or video outside your usual field, such as:

- a story of how a supply chain disruption affected multiple industries,
- an analysis of how environmental or policy changes ripple across economies,
- a case study of an ecosystem (natural or business) responding to unexpected shocks.

Jot a quick note: *What insight does this example give me about interconnectedness and hidden dependencies?*

ASK A STRATEGIC QUESTION   (~5 MIN)

Pick a current initiative and ask:

"If one critical element of this system were to fail, how would it affect the rest, and how would we respond?"

Capture your first thoughts; the goal is to train your mind to map dependencies before a crisis.

Whenever you face a meaningful decision, pause briefly:

"Does this action move us closer to where we want to be in 1–3 years?"

Record a quick yes/no or a few words explaining your reasoning.

END-OF-DAY CHECK

Circle the word that best describes your mindset tonight:

Clear   Curious   Stretched   Unsure   Energized

STRATEGIC TIP: If you circled *Curious* or *Unsure*, list one resource, an article, a mentor, a short video, you'll explore to help you move toward clarity.

Puzzle Piece	Fillable Statement
	I felt
	today because
	Before deciding what's next, I may need to
	(read, watch, ask, or reflect) to gain clarity.
	If you already know the next step, add:
	When I have that clarity, tomorrow I will

WHY IT MATTERS

Strategic thinkers anticipate dependencies and potential points of failure. Today's practice trains you to map those connections and prepare responses, so you can lead confidently even when the unexpected happens.

Day 32 – Systems Thinking

Strengthen your ability to anticipate how a change in one area can create ripple effects across people, processes, and results.

MORING PROMPT (~5 MIN)

Pause and write:

"What decision or shift under discussion today could create unexpected consequences in another department, team, or stakeholder group?"

Name the decision or shift and briefly describe where the ripple effects might occur.

....

....

SCAN THE HORIZON (~5–10 MIN)

Select and read, listen to, or watch one article, podcast, or short video outside your normal field, such as:

- a case study of how a small regulatory change reshaped multiple industries,
- a report on how technology adoption affects social or economic systems,
- an analysis of how one innovation disrupted an entire ecosystem.

Jot a sentence or two: *What insight does this give me about the way interconnected systems respond to change?*

....

ASK A STRATEGIC QUESTION (~5 MIN)

Select a current initiative and ask:

"If this change triggers an unexpected chain reaction, what early signs would tell us it's happening, and how would we adapt?"

Capture your first thoughts, don't worry about being precise; the aim is to build the habit of anticipating indirect effects.

....

Whenever you face a meaningful decision, pause briefly:

"Does this action move us closer to where we want to be in 1–3 years?"

Record a quick yes/no or a few words explaining your reasoning.

END-OF-DAY CHECK

Circle the word that best describes your mindset tonight:

Clear   Curious   Stretched   Unsure   Energized

STRATEGIC TIP: If you circled *Curious* or *Unsure*, list one resource, an article, a mentor, a short video, you'll explore to help you move toward clarity.

Puzzle Piece	Fillable Statement
	I felt
	today because
	Before deciding what's next, I may need to
	(read, watch, ask, or reflect) to gain clarity.
	If you already know the next step, add:
	When I have that clarity, tomorrow I will

WHY IT MATTERS

Strategic thinkers understand that complex systems rarely behave in straight lines. Today's practice trains you to look for early indicators of ripple effects so you can respond with foresight instead of surprise.

Day 33 — Systems Thinking

Practice mapping how decisions in one area influence outcomes across the entire organization or stakeholder network.

MORNING PROMPT (~5 MIN)

Pause and write:

"Which current initiative or decision relies on multiple teams or partners, and what could happen if one piece doesn't perform as expected?"

Identify the initiative and briefly describe the potential ripple effects.

SCAN THE HORIZON (~5–10 MIN)

Choose one article, podcast, or video outside your usual field, for example:

- a story about how a supply-chain failure disrupted multiple markets,
- a case study of how a local policy change triggered wider economic impacts,
- an analysis of how interconnected technologies amplified risk or opportunity.

Jot a sentence or two: What does this teach me about hidden dependencies or second-order consequences?

ASK A STRATEGIC QUESTION (~5 MIN)

Pick a current project or decision and ask:

"If one partner or key element failed without warning, how would it affect the rest of our system, and what contingency should we prepare now?"

Capture your first thoughts, don't aim for perfect answers; the goal is to strengthen your instinct for anticipating systemic risk.

Whenever a meaningful decision arises, pause briefly:

"Does this action move us closer to where we want to be in 1–3 years?"

Record a quick yes/no or a few words explaining your reasoning.

END-OF-DAY CHECK

Circle the word that best describes your mindset tonight:

Clear   **Curious**   **Stretched**   **Unsure**   **Energized**

STRATEGIC TIP: If you circled *Curious* or *Unsure*, list one resource, an article, a mentor, a short video, you'll explore to help you move toward clarity.

Puzzle Piece	Fillable Statement
	I felt
	today because
	Before deciding what's next, I may need to
	(read, watch, ask, or reflect) to gain clarity.
	If you already know the next step, add:
	When I have that clarity, tomorrow I will

WHY IT MATTERS

Strategic thinkers recognize that every system has critical connections and potential points of failure. Today's practice helps you identify those connections early so you can strengthen them, or plan contingencies, before disruption occurs.

Day 34 – Systems Thinking

Deepen your skill in anticipating how even small shifts can cascade through a larger system.

MORNING PROMPT (~5 MIN)

Pause and write:

"What small change or decision I'm aware of today could trigger a larger, unexpected consequence across our organization or stakeholders?"

Name the change or decision and briefly describe where the effects might show up.

SCAN THE HORIZON (~5–10 MIN)

Select and read, listen to, or watch one article, podcast, or short video outside your usual field, such as:

- a story about how a minor policy change disrupted an entire industry,
- an analysis of how one innovation altered multiple markets,
- a case study of an environmental ripple effect with broad consequences.

Jot a sentence or two: *What insight does this example offer about how complex systems react to small shifts?*

ASK A STRATEGIC QUESTION (~5 MIN)

Select a current project or initiative and ask:

"If this seemingly minor decision creates unexpected ripple effects, what early warning signs should we watch for, and how will we respond?"

Capture your first thoughts, don't worry about precision; the goal is to practice scanning for indirect impacts.

Whenever you face a meaningful decision, pause briefly:

"Does this action move us closer to where we want to be in 1–3 years?"

Record a quick yes/no or a few words explaining your reasoning.

END-OF-DAY CHECK

Circle the word that best describes your mindset tonight:

Clear   **Curious**   **Stretched**   **Unsure**   **Energized**

STRATEGIC TIP: If you circled Curious or Unsure, list one resource, an article, a mentor, a short video, you'll explore to help you move toward clarity.

Puzzle Piece	Fillable Statement
	I felt
	today because
	Before deciding what's next, I may need to
	(read, watch, ask, or reflect) to gain clarity.
	If you already know the next step, add:
	When I have that clarity, tomorrow I will

WHY IT MATTERS

Strategic thinkers know that small shifts can set off major consequences. Today's practice sharpens your awareness of those subtle starting points so you can anticipate, adapt, and guide your organization through complexity with confidence.

Day 35 — Systems Thinking

GOAL

Close the week by reflecting on the ripple effects you've noticed and the patterns that emerged from your systems-thinking practice.

MORNING PROMPT   (~5 MIN)

Pause and write:

"Looking back over the past week, what connection or dependency surprised me the most, and why?"

Name the connection and describe why it stood out.

SCAN THE HORIZON   (~5–10 MIN)

Select and read, listen to, or watch one article, podcast, or video outside your normal field, such as:

- a case study of how a small innovation disrupted multiple sectors,
- a story about global supply-chain dynamics,
- an analysis of how one event created second- and third-order effects.

Jot a sentence or two: What insight does this give me about anticipating ripple effects in my own work?

ASK A STRATEGIC QUESTION   (~5 MIN)

Pick a current initiative and ask:

"If one key element of our system unexpectedly failed or changed, what contingency would we need to activate first?"

Capture your first thoughts, this isn't about predicting perfectly, but about exercising the reflex to plan for interdependencies.

Whenever you face a meaningful decision, pause briefly:

"Does this action move us closer to where we want to be in 1–3 years?"

Record a quick yes/no or a few words explaining your reasoning.

END-OF-DAY CHECK

Circle the word that best describes your mindset tonight:

Clear   Curious   Stretched   Unsure   Energized

STRATEGIC TIP: If you circled *Curious* or *Unsure*, list one resource, an article, a mentor, a short video, you'll explore to help you move toward clarity.

Puzzle Piece	Fillable Statement
	I felt
	today because
	Before deciding what's next, I may need to
	(read, watch, ask, or reflect) to gain clarity.
	If you already know the next step, add:
	When I have that clarity, tomorrow I will

WHY IT MATTERS

Strategic thinkers understand that complex systems rarely behave in straight lines. Today's reflection helps you recognize the hidden connections you've uncovered and prepares you to lead with foresight when change creates unexpected ripple effects.

Week 5 Strategic Challenge – Systems Thinking

SCENARIO:

SCENARIO:

A small but critical vendor in your supply network suddenly announces a major policy shift.

It doesn't immediately affect your operations, but you sense it could create second- or third-order consequences over the next year.

YOUR TASK:

1. Identify three potential ripple effects this vendor change could cause across your organization or stakeholders.

....

....

2. List two key metrics or early indicators you would monitor to catch those ripple effects early.

....

....

3. Draft one proactive step you could take now to reduce the risk or seize any opportunity the change might create.

....

....

REFLECT:

- How does this exercise highlight the value of anticipating interdependencies?
- What habits from this week will help you stay alert to subtle signals of systemic change?

....

....

Explore additional scenarios and companion resources designed to deepen your use of the **ThinkSuite™ Strategic Intelligence Decks™**. *Visit www.pamelajgreen.com/store for details..*

Weekly Strategic Anchor

A Rhythm That Protects Your Progress

Strategic thinking isn't sustained by motivation, it's sustained by rhythm. Your Weekly Strategic Anchor is the one consistent ritual that keeps your goals, your focus, and your decisions aligned throughout the 66-day journey.

PURPOSE OF THE WEEKLY STRATEGIC ANCHOR

- Reconnect to your strategic priorities
- Review progress without judgment
- Anticipate obstacles before they derail you
- Recommit to the habits that matter most
- Make small adjustments that protect your long-term goals

Your anchor ensures you never drift too far from your intentions, even during busy or overwhelming weeks.

YOUR WEEKLY STRATEGIC ANCHOR RITUAL

Complete this every week on the same day, at the same time. Choose a moment that feels calm, available, and repeatable.

My Weekly Strategic Anchor Day & Time:

....

1. Strategic Wins This Week

What moved forward? What worked? List 2–3 wins, no matter how small.

....

....

2. What's Stuck or Slipping?

Identify challenges without blame. Awareness is your strategic leverage.

....

....

3. What Truly Mattered Most This Week?

Reflect on where your time, energy, and attention actually went.
The Three Priorities That Mattered Most:

1. ....

2. ....

3. ....

4. One Strategic Action for the Next 24 Hours

Choose the smallest meaningful action that moves your priority forward.

My One Action:
....

....

....

5. What Support or Resources Do I Need?

Strategic thinkers don't do it alone.

....

....

6. Alignment Check

Are my actions aligned with my long-term goals and values?

☐ Yes, keep going

☐ Not fully, what adjustment do I need to make?

Adjustment Needed (if any):

....

....

STRATEGIC INTEGRATION

"What does the strategic version of me need next week?"
Write your answer in one clear sentence:

....

....

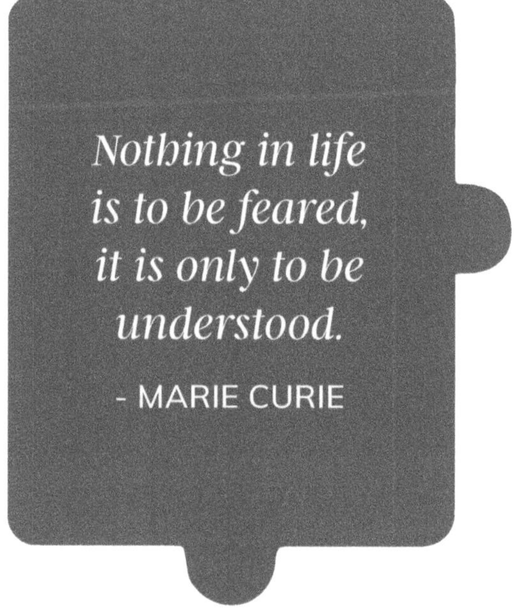

Nothing in life
is to be feared,
it is only to be
understood.

- MARIE CURIE

Day 36 — Trade-Offs

Start noticing that every strategic decision involves giving something up to gain something more important.

MORING PROMPT (~5 MIN)

Pause and write:

"What decision or priority on my plate today will require me, or my team, to say no to something else?"

Name the decision or priority and briefly describe what might need to be delayed, reduced, or declined.

....

....

SCAN THE HORIZON (~5–10 MIN)

Select and read, listen to, or watch one article, podcast, or short video outside your normal field, such as:

- a story about how a company chose long-term positioning over quick wins,
- an analysis of a public policy that forced hard budget choices,
- a case study of a leader who clearly articulated trade-offs to their team.

Jot a sentence or two: What insight does this example give me about the power, or the cost, of making clear trade-offs?

....

....

ASK A STRATEGIC QUESTION (~5 MIN)

Choose a current project or initiative and ask:

"If we choose this path, what are we intentionally saying no to, and what might we be saying no to without realizing it?"

Capture your first thoughts; the goal is to surface both the obvious and the hidden sacrifices.

....

Whenever a meaningful decision arises, pause briefly:

"Does this action move us closer to where we want to be in 1–3 years?"

Record a quick yes/no or a few words explaining your reasoning.

END-OF-DAY CHECK

Circle the word that best describes your mindset tonight:

Clear   Curious   Stretched   Unsure   Energized

STRATEGIC TIP: If you circled *Curious* or *Unsure*, list one resource, an article, a mentor, a short video, you'll explore to help you move toward clarity.

Puzzle Piece	Fillable Statement
	I felt ______________ today because ______________
	Before deciding what's next, I may need to ______________ (read, watch, ask, or reflect) to gain clarity.
	If you already know the next step, add: When I have that clarity, tomorrow I will ______________

WHY IT MATTERS

Strategic thinking is as much about choosing what not to do as it is about choosing what to pursue. Today's practice builds the discipline to recognize and name those trade-offs so that resources, energy, and attention are invested where they matter most.

Day 37 — Trade-Offs

GOAL

*Sharpen your ability to see both the gains **and** the sacrifices every strategic decision demands.*

MORNING PROMPT (~5 MIN)

Pause and write:

"Which priority or project today competes for resources with something equally important, and how will I decide which one wins?"

Name the competing priorities and briefly describe why the decision matters.

SCAN THE HORIZON (~5–10 MIN)

Select and read, listen to, or watch one short article, podcast, or video outside your usual field, for example:

- a case study of an organization that sacrificed short-term revenue for long-term impact,
- an analysis of a leader balancing innovation with budget constraints,
- a story of how clear trade-offs strengthened a company's brand or strategy.

Jot a quick note: *What lesson does this example give me about communicating or managing trade-offs?*

ASK A STRATEGIC QUESTION (~5 MIN)

Choose a current initiative and ask:

"If we fully fund or prioritize this effort, what must we delay, reduce, or decline, and what message does that send?"

Capture your first thoughts, don't worry about being precise; the aim is to make trade-offs explicit.

Whenever a meaningful decision arises, pause briefly:

"Does this action move us closer to where we want to be in 1–3 years?"

Record a quick yes/no or a few words capturing your reasoning.

END-OF-DAY CHECK

Circle the word that best describes your mindset tonight:

Clear   **Curious**   **Stretched**   **Unsure**   **Energized**

STRATEGIC TIP: If you circled *Curious* or *Unsure*, list one resource, an article, a mentor, a short video, you'll explore to help you move toward clarity.

Puzzle Piece	Fillable Statement
	I felt
	today because
	Before deciding what's next, I may need to
	(read, watch, ask, or reflect) to gain clarity.
	If you already know the next step, add:
	When I have that clarity, tomorrow I will

WHY IT MATTERS

Strategic leaders know that **every yes implies a no**. When a leader chooses to say yes to one priority, they are intentionally choosing not to pursue other options, even if those options are good, appealing, or popular. Your focus will require trade-offs.

Day 38 — Trade-Offs

GOAL

Notice where small, everyday choices quietly compete for your team's time, energy, and focus.

MORNING PROMPT   (~5 MIN)

Pause and write:

"Which routine activity or 'small' decision today could actually pull resources or attention away from our most important long-term goals?"

Name the activity or decision and briefly describe the potential cost.

....

....

SCAN THE HORIZON   (~5–10 MIN)

Select and read, listen to, or watch one article, podcast, or short video outside your usual field, for example:

- a story of a company that struggled because small inefficiencies compounded over time,
- an analysis of how minor policy choices created unexpected opportunity costs,
- a case of a leader who simplified operations by naming hidden trade-offs.

Jot a quick note: *What does this example teach me about the impact of small, often overlooked trade-offs?*

....

....

ASK A STRATEGIC QUESTION   (~5 MIN)

Pick a current project or decision and ask:

"If we keep investing in this small activity, what larger opportunity might we be unintentionally saying no to?"

Capture your first thoughts, don't aim for perfect answers; the goal is to surface hidden opportunity costs.

....

Whenever a meaningful decision arises, pause briefly:

"Does this action move us closer to where we want to be in 1–3 years?"

Record a quick yes/no or a few words summarizing your reasoning.

END-OF-DAY CHECK

Circle the word that best describes your mindset tonight:

Clear   **Curious**   **Stretched**   **Unsure**   **Energized**

STRATEGIC TIP: If you circled *Curious* or *Unsure*, list one resource, an article, a mentor, a short video, you'll explore to help you move toward clarity.

Puzzle Piece	Fillable Statement
	I felt
	today because
	Before deciding what's next, I may need to
	(read, watch, ask, or reflect) to gain clarity.
	If you already know the next step, add:
	When I have that clarity, tomorrow I will

WHY IT MATTERS

Strategic thinking means recognizing that even small yeses carry hidden no's. Today's practice helps you see where routine decisions quietly drain capacity so you can redirect attention and resources to what matters most.

Day 39 — Trade-Offs

Identify and evaluate the hidden costs of opportunities that look appealing at first glance.

MORNING PROMPT (~5 MIN)

Pause and write:

"What attractive opportunity or request on my radar today might carry hidden costs or unintended consequences if we say yes?"

Name the opportunity or request and briefly note the possible trade-offs.

....

....

SCAN THE HORIZON (~5–10 MIN)

Select and read, listen to, or watch one article, podcast, or short video outside your usual field, for example:

- a case study of a company that grew quickly but sacrificed long-term stability,
- an analysis of a public policy that delivered benefits with unexpected side effects,
- a story of a leader who turned down a tempting deal to stay true to strategy.

Jot a quick note: What does this example teach me about spotting hidden trade-offs before committing?

ASK A STRATEGIC QUESTION (~5 MIN)

Pick a current project or decision and ask:

"If we say yes to this opportunity, what must we delay, scale back, or decline, and what message does that send to our stakeholders?"

Capture your first thoughts, this isn't about having the perfect answer; it's about training your mind to weigh both the benefits and the costs.

....

Whenever you face a meaningful decision, pause briefly:

"Does this action move us closer to where we want to be in 1–3 years?"

Record a quick yes/no or a few words summarizing your reasoning.

END-OF-DAY CHECK

Circle the word that best describes your mindset tonight:

Clear   **Curious**   **Stretched**   **Unsure**   **Energized**

STRATEGIC TIP: If you circled *Curious* or *Unsure*, list one resource, an article, a mentor, a short video, you'll explore to help you move toward clarity.

Puzzle Piece	Fillable Statement
	I felt
	today because
	Before deciding what's next, I may need to
	(read, watch, ask, or reflect) to gain clarity.
	If you already know the next step, add:
	When I have that clarity, tomorrow I will

WHY IT MATTERS

Strategic thinkers know that **not every good opportunity is the right opportunity**. Today's practice sharpens your ability to uncover hidden costs and communicate the rationale for both yes and no decisions.

Day 40 – Trade-Offs

GOAL

Strengthen the habit of weighing long-term impact over short-term gain when making strategic decisions.

MORNING PROMPT   (~5 MIN)

Pause and write:

"Where am I tempted today to choose a quick win that could weaken our long-term strategy?"

Name the decision or situation and briefly describe why the short-term gain might be appealing.

....

....

SCAN THE HORIZON   (~5–10 MIN)

Select and read, listen to, or watch one article, podcast, or short video outside your usual field, such as:

* a case study of a company that sacrificed future strength for immediate results,
* an analysis of a public figure or leader who resisted pressure for quick wins,
* a story of how long-term discipline paid off in the face of short-term temptation.

Jot a sentence or two: *What insight does this example give me about staying committed to long-term priorities?*

....

....

ASK A STRATEGIC QUESTION   (~5 MIN)

Choose a current project or decision and ask:

"If we take the quick-win path, what long-term cost might we pay, and is that cost worth it?"

Capture your first thoughts, don't worry about getting it perfect; the goal is to surface potential trade-offs before acting.

....

Whenever a meaningful decision arises, pause briefly:

"Does this action move us closer to where we want to be in 1–3 years?"

Record a quick yes/no or a few words summarizing your reasoning.

END-OF-DAY CHECK

Circle the word that best describes your mindset tonight:

Clear   Curious   Stretched   Unsure   Energized

STRATEGIC TIP: If you circled *Curious* or *Unsure*, list one resource, an article, a mentor, a short video, you'll explore to help you move toward clarity.

Puzzle Piece	Fillable Statement
	I felt
	today because
	Before deciding what's next, I may need to
	(read, watch, ask, or reflect) to gain clarity.
	If you already know the next step, add:
	When I have that clarity, tomorrow I will

WHY IT MATTERS

Strategic thinking means **resisting the lure of quick wins when they undermine future success**. Today's practice reinforces the discipline to pause, weigh long-term costs, and make decisions that sustain lasting impact.

Day 41 – Trade-Offs

Refine your ability to name and communicate the trade-offs behind high-stakes decisions.

MORNING PROMPT (~5 MIN)

Pause and write:

"What decision or recommendation I'm making today requires me to explain what we're giving up, and how can I communicate that clearly?"

Identify the decision and briefly outline what will be sacrificed or delayed.

SCAN THE HORIZON (~5–10 MIN)

Select and read, listen to, or watch one article, podcast, or short video outside your usual field, such as:

- a case study of a leader who openly shared the costs of a strategic shift,
- an analysis of how clear communication-built trust during difficult choices,
- a story of how transparency about trade-offs strengthened stakeholder confidence.

Jot a quick note: What does this example teach me about explaining trade-offs without losing credibility or support?

ASK A STRATEGIC QUESTION (~5 MIN)

Pick a current initiative and ask:

"If stakeholders push back on the sacrifices we must make, how will I frame the long-term benefits so they see the value of our choice?"

Capture your first thoughts, focus on clarity and empathy.

Whenever a meaningful decision arises, pause briefly:

"Does this action move us closer to where we want to be in 1–3 years?"

Record a quick yes/no or a few words explaining your reasoning.

END-OF-DAY CHECK

Circle the word that best describes your mindset tonight:

Clear   **Curious**   **Stretched**   **Unsure**   **Energized**

STRATEGIC TIP: If you circled *Curious* or *Unsure*, list one resource, an article, a mentor, a short video, you'll explore to help you move toward clarity.

Puzzle Piece	Fillable Statement
	I felt
	today because
	Before deciding what's next, I may need to
	(read, watch, ask, or reflect) to gain clarity.
	If you already know the next step, add:
	When I have that clarity, tomorrow I will

WHY IT MATTERS

Strategic leaders not only make tough trade-offs, but they also communicate them in a way that builds trust. Today's practice helps you articulate both the sacrifice and the long-term payoff so others can stay engaged and committed.

Day 42 — Trade-Offs

GOAL

Pause to capture the lessons you've learned about balancing gains and sacrifices in strategic decision-making.

MORNING PROMPT (~5 MIN)

Pause and write:

"Looking back over this week, what trade-off did I notice, big or small, that will have the greatest long-term impact?"

Briefly describe the trade-off and why it stands out.

SCAN THE HORIZON (~5–10 MIN)

Select and read, listen to, or watch one short article, podcast, or video outside your usual field, such as:

- a case study of an organization that thrived by making a tough but wise sacrifice,
- an analysis of how clear trade-offs shaped an industry's future,
- a story of a leader whose long-term discipline paid off.

Jot a quick note: *What insight does this give me about making and communicating trade-offs?*

ASK A STRATEGIC QUESTION (~5 MIN)

Choose a current initiative and ask:

"If we fully commit to this decision, what do we need to consciously stop doing so our resources and attention stay focused?"

Write your first thoughts, don't worry about precision; the goal is to practice making trade-offs explicit.

Whenever a meaningful decision arises, pause briefly:

"Does this action move us closer to where we want to be in 1–3 years?"

In the space below, record a quick yes/no or a few words explaining your reasoning.

END-OF-DAY CHECK

Circle the word that best describes your mindset tonight:

Clear   **Curious**   **Stretched**   **Unsure**   **Energized**

STRATEGIC TIP: If you circled *Curious* or *Unsure*, list one resource, an article, a mentor, a short video, you'll explore to help you move toward clarity.

Puzzle Piece	Fillable Statement
	I felt
	today because
	Before deciding what's next, I may need to
	(read, watch, ask, or reflect) to gain clarity.
	If you already know the next step, add:
	When I have that clarity, tomorrow I will

WHY IT MATTERS

Strategic leaders know that every **significant choice carries a cost**. Capturing the week's most important trade-offs helps you reinforce the discipline of saying no with intention so your yes carries greater impact.

Week 6 Strategic Challenge — Trade-Offs

SCENARIO:

Your team receives an unexpected opportunity to secure significant funding if you can deliver a new product in half the planned time. Accepting the offer will require pulling resources from key long-term initiatives.

YOUR TASK:

1. List the **three most significant trade-offs** you would face if you accepted the offer.

....

....

2. Identify two **long-term risks** of saying yes, and two potential risks of saying no.

....

....

3. Draft the key message you would share with stakeholders to explain your decision.

....

....

REFLECT:

- How do you naturally weigh short-term rewards against long-term priorities?
- What habits from this week will help you communicate trade-offs with clarity and confidence in the future?

....

....

....

To continue sharpening your strategic thinking, explore more scenarios in the **ThinkSuite™ Strategic Intelligence Decks™**, *visit www.pamelajgreen.com/store for details.*

Weekly Strategic Anchor

A Rhythm That Protects Your Progress

Strategic thinking isn't sustained by motivation, it's sustained by rhythm.

Your Weekly Strategic Anchor is the one consistent ritual that keeps your goals, your focus, and your decisions aligned throughout the 66-day journey.

PURPOSE OF THE WEEKLY STRATEGIC ANCHOR

- Reconnect to your strategic priorities
- Review progress without judgment
- Anticipate obstacles before they derail you
- Recommit to the habits that matter most
- Make small adjustments that protect your long-term goals

Your anchor ensures you never drift too far from your intentions, even during busy or overwhelming weeks.

YOUR WEEKLY STRATEGIC ANCHOR RITUAL

Complete this every week on the same day, at the same time. Choose a moment that feels calm, available, and repeatable.

My Weekly Strategic Anchor Day & Time:

....

1. Strategic Wins This Week

What moved forward? What worked? List 2–3 wins, no matter how small.

....

....

2. What's Stuck or Slipping?

Identify challenges without blame. Awareness is your strategic leverage.

....

....

3. What Truly Mattered Most This Week?

Reflect on where your time, energy, and attention actually went.
The Three Priorities That Mattered Most:

1. ....

2. ....

3. ....

4. One Strategic Action for the Next 24 Hours

Choose the smallest meaningful action that moves your priority
forward.
My One Action:

....

....

5. What Support or Resources Do I Need?

Strategic thinkers don't do it alone.

....

....

6. Alignment Check

Are my actions aligned with my long-term goals and values?
☐ Yes, keep going
☐ Not fully, what adjustment do I need to make?
Adjustment Needed (if any):

....

....

STRATEGIC INTEGRATION

"What does the strategic version of me need next week?"
Write your answer in one clear sentence:

....

....

Phase 3 — Integration (Days 43–63)

By now you've built strong habits and tested them in action. Phase 3 helps you connect the dots and lead others:

Pattern Recognition

Scenario Thinking

Influence & Communication

Spotting signals and trends before the data shouts.

Asking "what if" so you can pivot when the unexpected arrives.

Framing messages so people understand not only what you're doing but why it matters.

Here you become not just a strategist but a storyteller, someone who turns insight into influence and invites others into the vision. These three weeks transform strategic thinking from a personal practice into a shared language of leadership.

Welcome to Week 7

The greatest
danger in times of
turbulence is not
the turbulence—
it is to act with
yesterday's logic.

- PETER DRUCKER

Day 43 — Pattern Recognition

Start noticing recurring signals, behaviors, or results that can reveal deeper strategic insights.

MORNING PROMPT (~5 MIN)

Pause and write:

"What repeated theme, challenge, or success have I noticed recently, and what might it be telling me about the bigger picture?"

Identify the pattern and briefly describe why it stands out.

SCAN THE HORIZON (~5–10 MIN)

Select and read, listen to, or watch one article, podcast, or short video outside your usual field, for example:

- a study on market or consumer behavior trends,
- a story of how data patterns revealed a new opportunity,
- an analysis of recurring geopolitical or economic shifts.

Jot a sentence or two: What pattern or lesson does this example highlight that might inform our own strategy?

ASK A STRATEGIC QUESTION (~5 MIN)

Choose a current project or initiative and ask:

"If this pattern continues or strengthens, what strategic move should we consider now?"

Capture your first thoughts, this isn't about certainty; it's about building the habit of seeing signals early.

STRATEGIC FILTER   (THROUGHOUT THE DAY)

Whenever a meaningful decision arises, pause briefly:

"Does this action move us closer to where we want to be in 1–3 years?"

Record a quick yes/no or a few words explaining your reasoning.

END-OF-DAY CHECK

Circle the word that best describes your mindset tonight:

Clear   **Curious**   **Stretched**   **Unsure**   **Energized**

STRATEGIC TIP: If you circled *Curious* or *Unsure*, list one resource, an article, a mentor, a short video, you'll explore to help you move toward clarity.

REFLECTION PROMPT:

What pattern did I notice today that I've seen before, and why might it be repeating?

WHY IT MATTERS

Strategic thinkers know that **patterns often reveal what data alone can't**. By training yourself to notice and interpret recurring signals, you gain an early advantage in spotting opportunities and risks.

Day 44 — Pattern Recognition

Sharpen your ability to connect recurring signals or events and draw insight from them.

MORNING PROMPT (~5 MIN)

Pause and write:

"What repeated challenge or opportunity has surfaced more than once in the past month, and what might it be signaling about our future?"

Name the recurring theme and briefly note why it catches your attention.

SCAN THE HORIZON (~5–10 MIN)

Select and read, listen to, or watch one article, podcast, or short video outside your usual field, for example:

- a report on emerging consumer habits,
- a study of how small recurring events reshaped an industry,
- a story of how a leader spotted a trend before it became obvious.

Jot a sentence or two: What pattern or trend does this example reveal that could influence our own strategy?

ASK A STRATEGIC QUESTION (~5 MIN)

Choose a current project or initiative and ask:

"If this pattern keeps showing up, what opportunity or risk might it be pointing to that we haven't yet addressed?"

Capture your first thoughts, don't worry about precision; the goal is to practice drawing insight from repetition.

STRATEGIC FILTER   (THROUGHOUT THE DAY)

Whenever a meaningful decision arises, pause briefly:

"Does this action move us closer to where we want to be in 1–3 years?"

Record a quick yes/no or a few words summarizing your reasoning.

END-OF-DAY CHECK

Circle the word that best describes your mindset tonight:

Clear   Curious   Stretched   Unsure   Energized

STRATEGIC TIP: If you circled *Curious* or *Unsure*, list one resource, an article, a mentor, a short video, you'll explore to help you move toward clarity.

REFLECTION PROMPT:

Where did I see a connection between two things I used to think were unrelated?

WHY IT MATTERS

Strategic thinkers recognize that **recurring signals often point to deeper forces at work**. By pausing to connect those dots, you position yourself to anticipate shifts and respond proactively rather than reactively.

Day 45 — Pattern Recognition

GOAL

Strengthen your habit of spotting relationships and trends that reveal strategic insight.

MORNING PROMPT (~5 MIN)

Pause and write:

"Which customer behavior, market signal, or internal trend have I seen more than once recently, and what might it be telling me about our long-term strategy?"

Name the pattern and briefly describe why it stands out.

SCAN THE HORIZON (~5–10 MIN)

Select and read, listen to, or watch one article, podcast, or short video outside your usual field, such as:

- a study of how repeated small shifts reshaped an entire market,
- a story of a leader who identified a trend before competitors,
- an analysis of data patterns that revealed hidden risks or opportunities.

Jot a sentence or two: What pattern in this example could inform how we plan or adapt?

ASK A STRATEGIC QUESTION (~5 MIN)

Choose a current project or decision and ask:

"If this pattern continues for the next year, how might it change our priorities or the way we allocate resources?"

Capture your first thoughts, don't worry about perfect answers; the aim is to link patterns to strategic decisions.

STRATEGIC FILTER (THROUGHOUT THE DAY)

Whenever you face a meaningful decision, pause briefly:

"Does this action move us closer to where we want to be in 1–3 years?"

Record a quick yes/no or a few words summarizing your reasoning.

END-OF-DAY CHECK

Circle the word that best describes your mindset tonight:

Clear   Curious   Stretched   Unsure   Energized

STRATEGIC TIP: If you circled *Curious* or *Unsure*, list one resource, an article, a mentor, a short video, you'll explore to help you move toward clarity.

REFLECTION PROMPT:

What trend, big or small, showed up today, and what might it be pointing toward?

WHY IT MATTERS

Strategic thinkers know that **patterns reveal emerging opportunities and risks** before the data is conclusive. Today's practice helps you connect recurring signals to potential strategic shifts, giving you a head start on proactive planning.

Day 46 — Pattern Recognition

GOAL

Deepen your ability to connect repeating signals or trends to meaningful strategic insights.

MORNING PROMPT   (~5 MIN)

Pause and write:

"What conversation, data point, or observation has surfaced multiple times this quarter, and what bigger story might it be telling?"

Identify the repeated signal and briefly describe why it might matter.

SCAN THE HORIZON   (~5–10 MIN)

Select and read, listen to, or watch one short article, podcast, or video outside your usual field, such as:

- a case study of how recurring weak signals predicted a market shift,
- a story of a leader who identified a turning point early,
- an analysis of patterns in policy or technology adoption.

Jot a sentence or two: What lesson does this example give me about spotting and interpreting patterns early?

ASK A STRATEGIC QUESTION   (~5 MIN)

Choose a current initiative and ask:

"If this pattern continues or accelerates, how should we adapt our strategy now to stay ahead?"

Capture your first thoughts, don't worry about precision; the aim is to practice translating patterns into action.

....

....

....

STRATEGIC FILTER (THROUGHOUT THE DAY)

Whenever a meaningful decision arises, pause briefly:

"Does this action move us closer to where we want to be in 1–3 years?"

Record a quick yes/no or a few words explaining your reasoning.

....

END-OF-DAY CHECK

Circle the word that best describes your mindset tonight:

Clear Curious Stretched Unsure Energized

STRATEGIC TIP: If you circled *Curious* or *Unsure*, list one resource, an article, a mentor, a short video, you'll explore to help you move toward clarity.

....

REFLECTION PROMPT:

Which recurring behavior (mine or others') influenced today's outcome?

....

....

....

....

WHY IT MATTERS

Strategic thinkers recognize that **recurring signals often point to forces shaping the future**. Today's practice builds your ability to detect these signals early and convert them into informed, proactive strategy.

Day 47 — Pattern Recognition

Sharpen your awareness of how recurring signals reveal opportunities or risks before they become obvious.

MORNING PROMPT (~5 MIN)

Pause and write:

"What pattern, across people, projects, or results, has caught my attention more than once this month, and what might it be pointing to?"

Identify the pattern and briefly describe why it stands out.

SCAN THE HORIZON (~5–10 MIN)

Select and read, listen to, or watch one article, podcast, or short video outside your normal field, such as:

- a story of how early patterns in customer behavior predicted a market shift,
- an analysis of repeated signals that preceded a major policy change,
- a case study of a leader who acted on emerging patterns before competitors.

Jot a sentence or two: What insight from this example can help me recognize or act on patterns earlier?

ASK A STRATEGIC QUESTION (~5 MIN)

Choose a current project or initiative and ask:

"If this pattern strengthens over the next six months, how would we need to adjust our priorities or strategy?"

Capture your first thoughts, don't aim for perfection; the goal is to practice connecting patterns to proactive action.

STRATEGIC FILTER   (THROUGHOUT THE DAY)

Whenever a meaningful decision arises, pause briefly:

"Does this action move us closer to where we want to be in 1–3 years?"

Record a quick yes/no or a few words summarizing your reasoning.

END-OF-DAY CHECK

Circle the word that best describes your mindset tonight:

Clear   Curious   Stretched   Unsure   Energized

STRATEGIC TIP: If you circled *Curious* or *Unsure*, list one resource, an article, a mentor, a short video, you'll explore to help you move toward clarity.

REFLECTION PROMPT:

What silent pattern surfaced, something people didn't say, but implied?

WHY IT MATTERS

Strategic thinkers know that **patterns often appear before the full story is visible**. Today's practice helps you spot these early signals and consider how they might reshape your long-term plans.

Day 48 — Pattern Recognition

Practice drawing insight from recurring signals so you can anticipate and shape future strategy.

MORNING PROMPT (~5 MIN)

Pause and write:

"Which repeated signal, inside or outside our organization, has started to feel too frequent to ignore, and what might it mean for our future direction?"

Identify the signal and briefly describe why it stands out now.

SCAN THE HORIZON (~5–10 MIN)

Select and read, listen to, or watch one article, podcast, or short video outside your normal field, such as:

- a case study where early patterns predicted a major shift in an industry,
- an analysis of recurring economic or social trends,
- a story of a leader who turned weak signals into a decisive strategic move.

Jot a sentence or two: What lesson does this example offer about acting on patterns before they become obvious?

ASK A STRATEGIC QUESTION (~5 MIN)

Choose a current initiative and ask:

"If this signal proves to be the start of a larger trend, what step should we take now to prepare or position ourselves?"

Capture your first thoughts, don't worry about getting it perfect; the goal is to connect early signals to early action.

....

....

....

Whenever you face a meaningful decision, pause briefly:

"Does this action move us closer to where we want to be in 1–3 years?"

Record a quick yes/no or a few words summarizing your reasoning.

....

END-OF-DAY CHECK

Circle the word that best describes your mindset tonight:

Clear   Curious   Stretched   Unsure   Energized

STRATEGIC TIP: If you circled *Curious* or *Unsure*, list one resource, an article, a mentor, a short video, you'll explore to help you move toward clarity.

....

REFLECTION PROMPT:

What did today reveal about how decisions ripple across systems or people?

....

....

....

WHY IT MATTERS

Strategic thinkers understand that **weak signals often become tomorrow's trends**. Today's practice strengthens your ability to notice when a pattern is gaining momentum and to prepare your organization to respond with foresight.

Day 49 — Pattern Recognition

Bring together the insights from your week of pattern spotting and decide how they can shape future strategy.

MORNING PROMPT (~5 MIN)

Pause and write:

"Looking back over this week, which pattern or recurring signal stands out as most important for our next 1–3 years, and why?"

Identify the pattern and briefly describe the strategic implications you see.

....

....

SCAN THE HORIZON (~5–10 MIN)

Select and read, listen to, or watch one short article, podcast, or video outside your normal field, such as:

- a story of how subtle market patterns predicted a significant shift,
- a report on long-term demographic or technological trends,
- an analysis of repeating signals that helped an organization plan.

Jot a sentence or two: What does this example teach me about acting early when patterns emerge?

....

....

....

ASK A STRATEGIC QUESTION (~5 MIN)

Choose a current project or initiative and ask:

"If this pattern continues or accelerates, what strategic move should we consider now to position ourselves for success?"

Capture your first thoughts, don't worry about being precise; the goal is to turn pattern recognition into strategic action.

STRATEGIC FILTER (THROUGHOUT THE DAY)

Whenever you face a meaningful decision, pause briefly:

"Does this action move us closer to where we want to be in 1–3 years?"

Record a quick yes/no or a few words summarizing your reasoning.

END-OF-DAY CHECK

Circle the word that best describes your mindset tonight:

Clear   Curious   Stretched   Unsure   Energized

STRATEGIC TIP: If you circled *Curious* or *Unsure*, list one resource, an article, a mentor, a short video, you'll explore to help you move toward clarity.

REFLECTION PROMPT:

Which pattern deserves my attention going forward, and why now?

WHY IT MATTERS

Strategic thinkers know that **the ability to connect dots across time and context creates competitive advantage**. Today's reflection helps you solidify your pattern-recognition practice and turn observations into concrete strategic options.

Week 7 Strategic Challenge – Pattern Recognition

SCENARIO:

Over the past quarter, customer feedback, market reports, and team conversations have all hinted, without stating outright, that a key product or service is losing relevance.

No single data point proves it, but the pattern is hard to ignore.

YOUR TASK:

1. List three indicators that, taken together, suggest the relevance issue might be real.

2. Draft two strategic questions you would pose to your leadership team to explore this possibility.

3. Identify one early, low-risk action you could take to test whether the pattern is valid (for example: pilot a new offering, run a small customer survey, or interview key clients).

REFLECT:

- How comfortable am I acting on patterns before I have complete data?
- What habits from this week will help me stay alert to weak signals and respond proactively?

Explore additional scenarios and companion resources designed to deepen your use of the **ThinkSuite™ Strategic Intelligence Decks™**. *Visit www.pamelajgreen.com/store for details.*

This Day 49 entry closes Week 7 by consolidating your pattern-recognition practice and offering a **fresh, journal-exclusive challenge** that strengthens the skill of turning subtle signals into strategic advantage.

Weekly Strategic Anchor

A Rhythm That Protects Your Progress

Strategic thinking isn't sustained by motivation, it's sustained by rhythm.

Your Weekly Strategic Anchor is the one consistent ritual that keeps your goals, your focus, and your decisions aligned throughout the 66-day journey.

PURPOSE OF THE WEEKLY STRATEGIC ANCHOR

- Reconnect to your strategic priorities
- Review progress without judgment
- Anticipate obstacles before they derail you
- Recommit to the habits that matter most
- Make small adjustments that protect your long-term goals

Your anchor ensures you never drift too far from your intentions, even during busy or overwhelming weeks.

YOUR WEEKLY STRATEGIC ANCHOR RITUAL

Complete this every week on the same day, at the same time. Choose a moment that feels calm, available, and repeatable.

My Weekly Strategic Anchor Day & Time:

....

1. Strategic Wins This Week

What moved forward? What worked? List 2–3 wins, no matter how small.

....

....

2. What's Stuck or Slipping?

Identify challenges without blame. Awareness is your strategic leverage.

....

....

3. What Truly Mattered Most This Week?

Reflect on where your time, energy, and attention actually went.
The Three Priorities That Mattered Most:

1.

2.

3.

4. One Strategic Action for the Next 24 Hours

Choose the smallest meaningful action that moves your priority forward.
My One Action:

5. What Support or Resources Do I Need?

Strategic thinkers don't do it alone.

6. Alignment Check

Are my actions aligned with my long-term goals and values?

☐ Yes, keep going

☐ Not fully, what adjustment do I need to make?

Adjustment Needed (if any):

STRATEGIC INTEGRATION

"What does the strategic version of me need next week?"
Write your answer in one clear sentence:

Learning is not attained by chance: it must be sought for with ardor and diligence.

\- ABIGAIL ADAMS

Day 50 – Scenario Thinking

Begin practicing "what if" thinking to prepare for multiple possible futures.

MORNING PROMPT (~5 MIN)

Pause and write:

"What important decision or initiative am I working on that could be disrupted if the future unfolds differently than expected?"

Name the initiative and briefly describe the kind of disruption you can imagine.

....

....

SCAN THE HORIZON (~5–10 MIN)

Select and read, listen to, or watch one **short article, podcast, or video outside your normal field**, such as:

- a story of an organization that prepared for multiple futures,
- a case study of a surprising market or policy shift,
- an analysis of how scenario planning revealed unexpected opportunities.

Jot a sentence or two: What lesson does this example give me about preparing for uncertainty?

....

....

....

ASK A STRATEGIC QUESTION (~5 MIN)

Choose a current project or decision and ask:

"If the opposite of our current assumptions became true tomorrow, what would we need to change immediately?"

Capture your first thoughts, don't worry about being exact; the goal is to stretch your imagination beyond the expected.

STRATEGIC FILTER (THROUGHOUT THE DAY)

Whenever a meaningful decision arises, pause briefly:

"Does this action move us closer to where we want to be in 1–3 years?"

Record a quick yes/no or a few words explaining your reasoning.

END-OF-DAY CHECK

Circle the word that best describes your mindset tonight:

Clear   Curious   Stretched   Unsure   Energized

STRATEGIC TIP: If you circled *Curious* or *Unsure*, list one resource, an article, a mentor, a short video, you'll explore to help you move toward clarity.

REFLECTION PROMPT:

If today's decision turned out differently than expected, what would the impact be?

WHY IT MATTERS

Strategic thinkers know that **the future rarely unfolds exactly as planned**. By considering alternate scenarios, even the opposite of what you expect, you build agility and position your organization to adapt quickly when reality shifts.

Day 51 — Scenario Thinking

Stretch your ability to imagine alternative futures and prepare for unexpected shifts.

MORNING PROMPT (~5 MIN)

Pause and write:

"If a major assumption we hold about our market, customers, or environment were suddenly proven wrong, what would change first?"

Identify the assumption and briefly describe the potential ripple effects.

....

....

SCAN THE HORIZON (~5–10 MIN)

Select and read, listen to, or watch one **short article, podcast, or video outside your usual field**, for example:

- a case study of a company surprised by a sudden market disruption,
- an analysis of how geopolitical or technological shifts changed the competitive landscape,
- a story of a leader who successfully anticipated an unexpected turn.

Jot a sentence or two: *What insight does this example give me about preparing for surprise?*

....

....

ASK A STRATEGIC QUESTION (~5 MIN)

Choose a current project or decision and ask:

"If the environment shifted dramatically in the next six months, what option would we wish we had already explored?"

Capture your first thoughts, this is about generating possibilities, not predicting perfectly.

STRATEGIC FILTER   (THROUGHOUT THE DAY)

Whenever a meaningful decision arises, pause briefly:

"Does this action move us closer to where we want to be in 1–3 years?"

Record a quick yes/no or a few words explaining your reasoning.

....

END-OF-DAY CHECK

Circle the word that best describes your mindset tonight:

Clear   Curious   Stretched   Unsure   Energized

STRATEGIC TIP: If you circled *Curious* or *Unsure*, list one resource, an article, a mentor, a short video, you'll explore to help you move toward clarity.

....

REFLECTION PROMPT:

What is one "opposite" scenario of a challenge I'm facing, and what does it teach me?

....

....

....

WHY IT MATTERS

Strategic thinkers understand that **resilience comes from considering multiple plausible futures**. Today's practice strengthens your ability to imagine disruptions early, so your organization can adapt quickly and confidently when reality changes.

Day 52 — Scenario Thinking

Strengthen your ability to anticipate multiple possible futures and prepare flexible responses.

MORNING PROMPT   (~5 MIN)

Pause and write:

"What event, inside or outside our industry, could unexpectedly accelerate or delay one of our key goals?"

Name the event you imagine and briefly describe how it could speed up or slow down progress.

SCAN THE HORIZON   (~5–10 MIN)

Select and read, listen to, or watch one article, **podcast, or short video outside your usual field**, such as:

- a case study of how a sudden technological breakthrough changed timelines,
- a story of how a policy shift disrupted long-term plans,
- an analysis of how unexpected market forces reshaped an industry.

Jot a sentence or two: *What lesson does this example give me about anticipating and preparing for shifting timelines?*

ASK A STRATEGIC QUESTION   (~5 MIN)

Choose a current project or decision and ask:

"If our timeline were cut in half, or doubled, how would we adjust our strategy right now?"

Capture your first thoughts, this isn't about predicting perfectly; it's about testing your flexibility.

....

....

STRATEGIC FILTER   (THROUGHOUT THE DAY)

Whenever a meaningful decision arises, pause briefly:

"Does this action move us closer to where we want to be in 1–3 years?"

Record a quick yes/no or a few words explaining your reasoning.

....

END-OF-DAY CHECK

Circle the word that best describes your mindset tonight:

Clear   Curious   Stretched   Unsure   Energized

STRATEGIC TIP: If you circled *Curious* or *Unsure*, list one resource, an article, a mentor, a short video, you'll explore to help you move toward clarity.

....

REFLECTION PROMPT:

If the best-case scenario happened, what would need to be true?

....

....

....

WHY IT MATTERS

Strategic thinkers know that **uncertainty can accelerate or slow down plans without warning**.

Today's practice builds the habit of stress-testing your strategy against different timelines so you can respond quickly, without losing focus on the long-term vision.

Day 53 — Scenario Thinking

Build the habit of considering alternative outcomes so you can adapt before disruption forces your hand.

MORNING PROMPT (~5 MIN)

Pause and write:

"If a key partner, vendor, or stakeholder suddenly changed direction, how would it affect our current strategy?"

Name the partner or stakeholder and briefly describe the potential impact.

SCAN THE HORIZON (~5–10 MIN)

Select and read, listen to, or watch one article, **podcast, or short video outside your normal field**, such as:

- a story of a partnership breakdown that reshaped an industry,
- a case study of how a sudden policy or regulatory change disrupted key alliances,
- an analysis of how a supply chain pivot created unexpected opportunities.

Jot a sentence or two: What lesson does this example give me about preparing for unexpected shifts in relationships or dependencies?

ASK A STRATEGIC QUESTION (~5 MIN)

Choose a current project or decision and ask:

"If this key partner or stakeholder took a different path tomorrow, what immediate step would we need to take to protect our strategy?"

Capture your first thoughts, don't worry about perfect answers; the goal is to practice contingency thinking.

....

....

....

Whenever a meaningful decision arises, pause briefly:

"Does this action move us closer to where we want to be in 1–3 years?"

Record a quick yes/no or a few words explaining your reasoning.

....

END-OF-DAY CHECK

Circle the word that best describes your mindset tonight:

Clear   Curious   Stretched   Unsure   Energized

STRATEGIC TIP: If you circled *Curious* or *Unsure*, list one resource, an article, a mentor, a short video, you'll explore to help you move toward clarity.

....

REFLECTION PROMPT:

If the worst-case scenario happened, where am I most vulnerable?

....

....

....

WHY IT MATTERS

Strategic thinkers recognize that **external relationships can shift suddenly and reshape your plans**. Today's practice helps you anticipate those possibilities and identify early moves that protect your strategy and create new options.

Day 54 — Scenario Thinking

Practice imagining multiple futures so you can respond with agility when reality shifts.

MORNING PROMPT   (~5 MIN)

Pause and write:

"If an unexpected economic or industry shock occurred next quarter, which part of our strategy would be most vulnerable, and why?"

Identify the vulnerable area and briefly describe why it could be affected first.

SCAN THE HORIZON   (~5–10 MIN)

Select and read, listen to, or watch one article, **podcast, or short video outside your normal field**, such as:

- a case study of how an unforeseen crisis reshaped a market,
- a story of a company that pivoted quickly after an economic downturn,
- an analysis of how sudden policy changes disrupted long-term plans.

Jot a sentence or two: What lesson does this example give me about building resilience into our plans?

ASK A STRATEGIC QUESTION   (~5 MIN)

Choose a current project or decision and ask:

"If we had to adapt to a sudden downturn or shock, what is the first action we would need to take to safeguard our mission and long-term goals?"

Capture your first thoughts, don't worry about getting it perfect; the goal is to explore contingency planning.

Whenever a meaningful decision arises, pause briefly:

"Does this action move us closer to where we want to be in 1–3 years?"

Record a quick yes/no or a few words explaining your reasoning.

END-OF-DAY CHECK

Circle the word that best describes your mindset tonight:

Clear   Curious   Stretched   Unsure   Energized

STRATEGIC TIP: If you circled *Curious* or *Unsure*, list one resource, an article, a mentor, a short video, you'll explore to help you move toward clarity.

REFLECTION PROMPT:

What scenario am I not considering because it feels unlikely, but still matters?

WHY IT MATTERS

Strategic thinkers know that **crises rarely announce themselves in advance**.

Today's practice strengthens your capacity to envision sudden shocks and prepare early moves that protect long-term strategy and build resilience.

Day 55 – Scenario Thinking

Strengthen your ability to rehearse alternative futures so you can adapt when reality surprises you.

MORNING PROMPT (~5 MIN)

Pause and write:

"If customer or stakeholder expectations shifted dramatically next quarter, how would our current strategy need to adapt?"

Identify the expectation you imagine changing and briefly describe the possible impact.

....

....

SCAN THE HORIZON (~5–10 MIN)

Select and read, listen to, or watch one article, **podcast, or short video outside your usual field,** such as:

- a case study of how changing customer behaviors reshaped a business model,
- an analysis of sudden shifts in public sentiment,
- a story of a leader who quickly repositioned after a dramatic change in stakeholder expectations.

Jot a sentence or two: *What lesson does this example give me about staying agile when expectations evolve?*

....

....

ASK A STRATEGIC QUESTION (~5 MIN)

Choose a current project or decision and ask:

"If expectations change in a way we don't anticipate, what is one proactive step we can take today to stay ahead?"

Capture your first thoughts, don't worry about precision; the goal is to explore options before change forces your hand.

....

....

....

STRATEGIC FILTER   (THROUGHOUT THE DAY)

Whenever a meaningful decision arises, pause briefly:

"Does this action move us closer to where we want to be in 1–3 years?"

Record a quick yes/no or a few words explaining your reasoning.

....

END-OF-DAY CHECK

Circle the word that best describes your mindset tonight:

Clear   Curious   Stretched   Unsure   Energized

STRATEGIC TIP: If you circled *Curious* or *Unsure*, list one resource, an article, a mentor, a short video, you'll explore to help you move toward clarity.

....

REFLECTION PROMPT:

Who would be most impacted by alternate scenarios, and how should that shape my choices?

....

....

....

WHY IT MATTERS

Strategic thinkers know that **customer and stakeholder expectations can pivot overnight**.

Today's practice builds the habit of exploring "what if" shifts in sentiment so you can adjust your strategy before the pressure mounts.

Day 56 — Scenario Thinking

Consolidate what you've learned about preparing for multiple futures and acting with agility when conditions change.

MORNING PROMPT   (~5 MIN)

Pause and write:

"Looking back over this week, what scenario or 'what if' question challenged my assumptions the most, and what did I learn from it?"

Name the scenario and briefly describe the key insight.

....

....

SCAN THE HORIZON   (~5–10 MIN)

Select and read, listen to, or watch one short article, **podcast, or video outside your normal field**, such as:

- a story of how scenario planning helped an organization thrive through disruption,
- an analysis of a surprising market or policy shift,
- a case study of leaders who prepared for multiple futures and gained advantage.

Jot a sentence or two: What lesson does this example give me about the value of rehearsing multiple futures?

....

....

ASK A STRATEGIC QUESTION   (~5 MIN)

Choose a current initiative and ask:

"If the future takes a very different path than expected, what is one strategic option we should start exploring now?"

Capture your first thoughts, this isn't about predicting perfectly; it's about keeping options open.

STRATEGIC FILTER   (THROUGHOUT THE DAY)

Whenever a meaningful decision arises, pause briefly:

"Does this action move us closer to where we want to be in 1–3 years?"

Record a quick yes/no or a few words explaining your reasoning.

END-OF-DAY CHECK

Circle the word that best describes your mindset tonight:

Clear   Curious   Stretched   Unsure   Energized

STRATEGIC TIP: If you circled *Curious* or *Unsure*, list one resource, an article, a mentor, a short video, you'll explore to help you move toward clarity.

REFLECTION PROMPT:

Where can I reduce risk or increase opportunity based on what today revealed?

WHY IT MATTERS

Strategic thinkers understand that **resilience grows when you explore multiple plausible futures**. Reflecting on this week's scenarios helps you internalize the practice of asking "what if" and equips you to adapt confidently when reality diverges from the plan.

Week 8 Strategic Challenge – Scenario Thinking

SCENARIO:

A sudden global event, such as a regulatory shift, technological breakthrough, or geopolitical disruption, has the potential to upend your industry in the next 12 months.

You have only early signals and no clear timeline.

YOUR TASK:

1. Outline **three distinct scenarios** (best case, worst case, and most likely) for how this event could unfold.

2. Identify **two strategic moves** you would make today that would be valuable across all three scenarios.

3. Draft a brief message to your team explaining why you are preparing for multiple futures and how this strengthens the organization.

REFLECT:

- How comfortable am I making decisions amid uncertainty?
- What habits from this week will help me remain agile when the future refuses to follow the plan?

To continue sharpening your strategic thinking, explore more scenarios in the **ThinkSuite™ Strategic Intelligence Decks™**, *visit www.pamelajgreen.com/store for details.*

Weekly Strategic Anchor

A Rhythm That Protects Your Progress

Strategic thinking isn't sustained by motivation, it's sustained by rhythm.

Your Weekly Strategic Anchor is the one consistent ritual that keeps your goals, your focus, and your decisions aligned throughout the 66-day journey.

PURPOSE OF THE WEEKLY STRATEGIC ANCHOR

- Reconnect to your strategic priorities
- Review progress without judgment
- Anticipate obstacles before they derail you
- Recommit to the habits that matter most
- Make small adjustments that protect your long-term goals

Your anchor ensures you never drift too far from your intentions, even during busy or overwhelming weeks.

YOUR WEEKLY STRATEGIC ANCHOR RITUAL

Complete this every week on the same day, at the same time. Choose a moment that feels calm, available, and repeatable.

My Weekly Strategic Anchor Day & Time:

....

1. Strategic Wins This Week

What moved forward? What worked? List 2–3 wins, no matter how small.

....

....

2. What's Stuck or Slipping?

Identify challenges without blame. Awareness is your strategic leverage.

....

....

3. What Truly Mattered Most This Week?

Reflect on where your time, energy, and attention actually went. The Three Priorities That Mattered Most:

1.

2.

3.

4. One Strategic Action for the Next 24 Hours

Choose the smallest meaningful action that moves your priority forward.

My One Action:

5. What Support or Resources Do I Need?

Strategic thinkers don't do it alone.

6. Alignment Check

Are my actions aligned with my long-term goals and values?

☐ Yes, keep going

☐ Not fully, what adjustment do I need to make?

Adjustment Needed (if any):

STRATEGIC INTEGRATION

"What does the strategic version of me need next week?"
Write your answer in one clear sentence:

Welcome to Week 9

> *Great leaders don't guess. They gather the right data and use it to make better decisions.*
>
> - BRAD SMART

Day 57 — Influence & Communication

Begin refining how you frame messages so others see the strategic "why," not just the tactical "what."

MORNING PROMPT   (~5 MIN)

Pause and write:

"What message, presentation, or conversation do I have today that needs to clearly show why this matters for our long-term strategy?"

Identify the message and briefly note why conveying the long-term "why" is critical.

SCAN THE HORIZON   (~5–10 MIN)

Select and read, listen to, or watch one article, **podcast, or short video outside your usual field**, such as:

- a case study of a leader who inspired action by framing a long-term vision,
- an analysis of how clear strategic messaging built stakeholder trust,
- a story of an organization whose communication shifted culture or strategy.

Jot a sentence or two: *What does this example teach me about linking day-to-day communication to long-term goals?*

ASK A STRATEGIC QUESTION   (~5 MIN)

Choose a current project or decision and ask:

"If I had to explain why this matters for our future in just one sentence, what would I say?"

Capture your first thoughts, focus on clarity and impact, not perfection.

STRATEGIC FILTER   (THROUGHOUT THE DAY)

Whenever a meaningful decision arises, pause briefly:

"Does this action move us closer to where we want to be in 1–3 years?"

Record a quick yes/no or a few words explaining your reasoning.

END-OF-DAY CHECK

Circle the word that best describes your mindset tonight:

Clear   Curious   Stretched   Unsure   Energized

STRATEGIC TIP: If you circled *Curious* or *Unsure*, list one resource, an article, a mentor, a short video, you'll explore to help you move toward clarity.

REFLECTION PROMPT:

How did I influence someone's thinking today, and was that influence intentional?

WHY IT MATTERS

Strategic thinkers know that **influence comes from showing how today's actions connect to tomorrow's vision**. Today's practice helps you frame your messages so people understand not only what you're asking, but also why it matters for the future.

Day 58 — Influence & Communication

Strengthen your ability to communicate the long-term value of your decisions so others see the bigger picture.

MORNING PROMPT   (~5 MIN)

Pause and write:

"What conversation or message today gives me the best opportunity to connect a short-term action to our long-term vision?"

Identify the conversation or message and briefly note why linking it to the vision will matter.

SCAN THE HORIZON   (~5–10 MIN)

Select and read, listen to, or watch one article, **podcast, or short video outside your usual field**, such as:

- a story of a leader who rallied support by framing a bold future,
- an analysis of how strategic communication built confidence during change,
- a case study of a team that stayed united through clear and inspiring messaging.

Jot a sentence or two: What insight from this example can I apply to make my own communication more future-focused?

ASK A STRATEGIC QUESTION   (~5 MIN)

Choose a current project or decision and ask:

"If I want people to fully commit to this initiative, how can I clearly explain why it matters for our success 1–3 years from now?"

Capture your first thoughts, focus on clarity and resonance, not perfection.

....

....

....

STRATEGIC FILTER   (THROUGHOUT THE DAY)

Whenever a meaningful decision arises, pause briefly:

"Does this action move us closer to where we want to be in 1–3 years?"

Record a quick yes/no or a few words explaining your reasoning.

....

END-OF-DAY CHECK

Circle the word that best describes your mindset tonight:

Clear   Curious   Stretched   Unsure   Energized

STRATEGIC TIP: If you circled *Curious* or *Unsure*, list one resource, an article, a mentor, a short video, you'll explore to help you move toward clarity.

....

REFLECTION PROMPT:

What message did I communicate today that helped others see the bigger picture?

....

....

....

WHY IT MATTERS

Strategic leaders know that **people commit when they understand the future impact of today's actions**. Today's practice builds your skill in linking immediate tasks to long-term goals, so others are inspired to act with you.

Day 59 — Influence & Communication

Refine your ability to inspire action by framing messages around purpose and long-term impact.

MORNING PROMPT　　(~5 MIN)

Pause and write:

"Which team, stakeholder, or partner most needs to hear why our current work matters for the future, and what key point will resonate most with them?"

Identify the audience and briefly note the long-term value you want them to see.

SCAN THE HORIZON　　(~5–10 MIN)

Select and read, listen to, or watch one **article, podcast, or short video outside your usual field**, such as:

- a case study of a leader who galvanized support through compelling storytelling,
- an analysis of how clear vision messaging united diverse stakeholders,
- a story of an organization whose communication built trust in uncertain times.

Jot a sentence or two: What lesson from this example can strengthen how I communicate our strategic purpose?

ASK A STRATEGIC QUESTION　　(~5 MIN)

Choose a current initiative and ask:

"If I had only one minute to convince this audience of our long-term goal, what would I say to inspire confidence and action?"

Capture your first thoughts, focus on clarity and emotional connection.

　　

....

....

....

STRATEGIC FILTER   (THROUGHOUT THE DAY)

Whenever a meaningful decision arises, pause briefly:

"Does this action move us closer to where we want to be in 1–3 years?"

Record a quick yes/no or a few words explaining your reasoning.

....

END-OF-DAY CHECK

Circle the word that best describes your mindset tonight:

Clear   Curious   Stretched   Unsure   Energized

STRATEGIC TIP: If you circled *Curious* or *Unsure*, list one resource, an article, a mentor, a short video, you'll explore to help you move toward clarity.

....

REFLECTION PROMPT:

Where might I have missed an opportunity to communicate strategically?

....

....

....

....

WHY IT MATTERS

Strategic thinkers know that **influence grows when others clearly see the future impact of today's work**. Today's practice helps you translate strategic goals into a message that motivates people to join you in shaping the long-term vision.

Day 60 — Influence & Communication

Strengthen your skill in framing messages so people understand both the logic and the long-term benefit of your decisions.

MORNING PROMPT (~5 MIN)

Pause and write:

"What key decision or update today needs to be explained in a way that shows how it protects or advances our long-term goals?"

Identify the decision or update and briefly describe the strategic benefit you need to highlight.

SCAN THE HORIZON (~5–10 MIN)

Select and read, listen to, or watch one **article, podcast, or short video outside your usual field**, such as:

- a case study of a leader who maintained trust during a controversial decision,
- an analysis of how transparent communication built long-term credibility,
- a story of an organization whose strategic messaging kept stakeholders engaged through change.

Jot a sentence or two: What lesson does this example give me about building trust while explaining long-term strategy?

ASK A STRATEGIC QUESTION (~5 MIN)

Choose a current initiative and ask:

"If stakeholders question this decision, how can I clearly link it to our vision for the next 1–3 years?"

Capture your first thoughts, focus on clarity and connection.

STRATEGIC FILTER (THROUGHOUT THE DAY)

Whenever a meaningful decision arises, pause briefly:

"Does this action move us closer to where we want to be in 1–3 years?"

Record a quick yes/no or a few words explaining your reasoning.

END-OF-DAY CHECK

Circle the word that best describes your mindset tonight:

Clear   **Curious**   **Stretched**   **Unsure**   **Energized**

STRATEGIC TIP: If you circled *Curious* or *Unsure*, list one resource, an article, a mentor, a short video, you'll explore to help you move toward clarity.

REFLECTION PROMPT:

Whose perspective did I seek today, and how did it shape my understanding?

WHY IT MATTERS

Strategic leaders understand that **influence comes from connecting decisions to a clear long-term purpose**. Today's practice helps you communicate not just what you decided, but why it matters, building trust and commitment among those you lead.

Day 61 – Influence & Communication

GOAL

Deepen your ability to inspire action by showing how today's work connects to tomorrow's vision.

MORNING PROMPT   (~5 MIN)

Pause and write:

"Who most needs to hear today how their work contributes to our long-term strategy, and what specific words will make that connection clear?"

Identify the person or group and briefly describe the message you want to convey.

SCAN THE HORIZON   (~5–10 MIN)

Select and read, listen to, or watch one **article, podcast, or short video outside your usual field**, such as:

- a story of a leader who strengthened engagement by highlighting each person's role in the bigger picture,
- an analysis of how strategic storytelling unified diverse teams,
- a case study of an organization whose leaders consistently tied daily tasks to long-term outcomes.

Jot a sentence or two: What insight does this example give me about helping others see their role in the future vision?

ASK A STRATEGIC QUESTION   (~5 MIN)

Choose a current initiative and ask:

"If every team member clearly understood how their work supports the 1–3 year strategy, what difference would it make in execution and morale?"

Capture your first thoughts, focus on the impact of clarity and shared purpose.

STRATEGIC FILTER (THROUGHOUT THE DAY)

Whenever a meaningful decision arises, pause briefly:

"Does this action move us closer to where we want to be in 1–3 years?"

Record a quick yes/no or a few words explaining your reasoning.

....

END-OF-DAY CHECK

Circle the word that best describes your mindset tonight:

Clear   Curious   Stretched   Unsure   Energized

STRATEGIC TIP: If you circled *Curious* or *Unsure*, list one resource, an article, a mentor, a short video, you'll explore to help you move toward clarity.

....

REFLECTION PROMPT:

How did I frame an idea or decision today so others could understand its long-term value?

....

....

....

WHY IT MATTERS

Strategic leaders know that **people give their best when they see how their daily efforts shape the organization's future**. Today's practice helps you communicate that connection so others are motivated and aligned with the long-term vision.

Day 62 — Influence & Communication

Refine the way you frame messages, so they build trust and reinforce the organization's long-term vision.

MORNING PROMPT (~5 MIN)

Pause and write:

"What decision or update today could easily be misunderstood if I don't clearly connect it to our long-term strategy?"

Identify the decision or update and briefly note why careful framing matters.

....

....

SCAN THE HORIZON (~5–10 MIN)

Select and read, listen to, or watch one **article, podcast, or short video outside your usual field**, such as:

- a case study of a leader who maintained trust during a controversial change,
- an analysis of how transparent messaging shaped stakeholder confidence,
- a story of how a clear narrative helped an organization navigate uncertainty.

Jot a sentence or two: What lesson does this example give me about communicating complex decisions with clarity and purpose?

....

....

ASK A STRATEGIC QUESTION (~5 MIN)

Choose a current initiative and ask:

"If stakeholders question this decision, how can I explain it in a way that reinforces our shared 1–3 year vision?"

Capture your first thoughts, focus on clarity and reassurance.

STRATEGIC FILTER   (THROUGHOUT THE DAY)

Whenever a meaningful decision arises, pause briefly:

"Does this action move us closer to where we want to be in 1–3 years?"

Record a quick yes/no or a few words explaining your reasoning.

....

END-OF-DAY CHECK

Circle the word that best describes your mindset tonight:

Clear   Curious   Stretched   Unsure   Energized

STRATEGIC TIP: If you circled *Curious* or *Unsure*, list one resource, an article, a mentor, a short video, you'll explore to help you move toward clarity.

....

REFLECTION PROMPT:

Which stakeholder or team member needs more clarity from me, and what will I say tomorrow?

....

....

....

WHY IT MATTERS

Strategic leaders understand that **how you explain a decision can matter as much as the decision itself**. Today's practice helps you communicate with transparency and align people to the bigger picture, especially when the message is complex or sensitive.

Day 63 — Influence & Communication

Capture the lessons you've learned about using communication to inspire and align people around long-term goals.

MORNING PROMPT   (~5 MIN)

Pause and write:

"Looking back over this week, what conversation or message most successfully connected our daily work to our long-term vision, and why did it resonate?"

Briefly describe the conversation or message and note the key factors that made it effective.

....

....

SCAN THE HORIZON   (~5–10 MIN)

Select and read, listen to, or watch one **article, podcast, or short video outside your normal field**, such as:

- a story of a leader whose compelling narrative transformed organizational culture,
- an analysis of how consistent strategic messaging builds trust through change,
- a case study of how visionary communication rallied people behind a bold goal.

Jot a sentence or two: What does this example teach me about sustaining influence through clear, future-focused communication?

....

....

ASK A STRATEGIC QUESTION   (~5 MIN)

Choose a current initiative and ask:

"If we want our long-term strategy to stay alive in daily conversations, what one communication habit should we practice consistently?"

Capture your first thoughts, focus on habits that make the strategic vision part of everyday language.

....

....

STRATEGIC FILTER   (THROUGHOUT THE DAY)

Whenever a meaningful decision arises, pause briefly:

"Does this action move us closer to where we want to be in 1–3 years?"

Record a quick yes/no or a few words explaining your reasoning.

....

END-OF-DAY CHECK

Circle the word that best describes your mindset tonight:

Clear   Curious   Stretched   Unsure   Energized

STRATEGIC TIP: If you circled *Curious* or *Unsure*, list one resource, an article, a mentor, a short video, you'll explore to help you move toward clarity.

....

REFLECTION PROMPT:

What did I do today that strengthened alignment around a shared goal?

....

....

....

WHY IT MATTERS

Strategic thinkers know that **influence is sustained by consistently linking today's actions to tomorrow's vision.** Today's reflection helps you identify which messages and habits most effectively inspire others and keep the strategic vision front and center.

Week 9 Strategic Challenge – Influence & Communication

SCENARIO:

Your organization is about to announce a significant strategic shift that could unsettle employees and key stakeholders. Some will be excited; others will be anxious or skeptical.

YOUR TASK:

1. Draft the **three most important points** you must convey to ensure people understand the purpose and long-term value of the shift.

2. Identify two different audiences (for example, staff and board members) and outline how you would tailor the message for each.

3. Write one powerful closing sentence that reinforces confidence and unites everyone behind the strategy.

REFLECT:

- What communication habits from this week will help me guide others through this transition?
- How can I keep the long-term vision visible even when short-term uncertainty arises?

To continue sharpening your strategic thinking, explore more scenarios in the **ThinkSuite™ Strategic Intelligence Decks™**, *visit www.pamelajgreen.com/store for details.*

Weekly Strategic Anchor

A Rhythm That Protects Your Progress

Strategic thinking isn't sustained by motivation, it's sustained by rhythm.

Your Weekly Strategic Anchor is the one consistent ritual that keeps your goals, your focus, and your decisions aligned throughout the 66-day journey.

PURPOSE OF THE WEEKLY STRATEGIC ANCHOR

- Reconnect to your strategic priorities
- Review progress without judgment
- Anticipate obstacles before they derail you
- Recommit to the habits that matter most
- Make small adjustments that protect your long-term goals

Your anchor ensures you never drift too far from your intentions, even during busy or overwhelming weeks.

YOUR WEEKLY STRATEGIC ANCHOR RITUAL

Complete this every week on the same day, at the same time. Choose a moment that feels calm, available, and repeatable.

My Weekly Strategic Anchor Day & Time:

....

1. Strategic Wins This Week

What moved forward? What worked? List 2–3 wins, no matter how small.

....

....

2. What's Stuck or Slipping?

Identify challenges without blame. Awareness is your strategic leverage.

....

....

3.   What Truly Mattered Most This Week?

Reflect on where your time, energy, and attention actually went.
The Three Priorities That Mattered Most:

1.
....
2.
....
3.
....

4.   One Strategic Action for the Next 24 Hours

Choose the smallest meaningful action that moves your priority forward.
My One Action:

....

....

5.   What Support or Resources Do I Need?

Strategic thinkers don't do it alone.

....

....

6. Alignment Check

Are my actions aligned with my long-term goals and values?

☐ Yes, keep going

☐ Not fully, what adjustment do I need to make?

Adjustment Needed (if any):

....

....

STRATEGIC INTEGRATION

"What does the strategic version of me need next week?"
Write your answer in one clear sentence:

....

....

                                                          ©2026 Pamela J. Green

Congratulations! You've made it to Phase 4: Mastery.

PAUSE

The discipline of stopping the automatic response to create space for clarity. This step interrupts urgency, emotion, and overthinking.

THINK

Intentional inquiry using strategic lenses that expand perspective. This includes asking better questions, scanning the horizon, and building insight.

GROW

Personal and professional growth through alignment, better decisions, and mindset expansion.

STRATEGICALLY

Embedding strategic thinking into daily leadership practice until it becomes identity. This is where the 66 days turns habit into leadership reflex.

The Final Stretch — Mastery & Beyond (Days 64–66)

Sustaining Your Strategic Habits

You've arrived at the final days of the journey, but this is really the beginning of a lifelong practice. The final stretch is about mastery and momentum:

- Blending all five habits, future focus, systems thinking, pattern recognition, scenario thinking, and influential communication, into a single leadership reflex.
- Crafting your personal 90-day plan to keep these habits alive.
- Identifying the accountability structures, coaches, peers, or simple check-ins, that will help you stay the course.

Celebrate how far you've come. Strategic thinking is no longer an event or a checklist; it's becoming who you are as a leader. As you step beyond these pages, keep pausing intentionally, thinking strategically, and growing the influence that only you can bring.

Day 64 — Mastery & Integration

GOAL

Begin blending the habits you've built, future focus, systems thinking, pattern recognition, scenario planning, and influence, into a single, natural leadership practice.

MORNING PROMPT   (~5 MIN)

Pause and write:

"Which strategic habit I've developed over the past nine weeks has influenced my thinking the most, and how can I use it today?"

Identify the habit and briefly describe how you'll apply it.

SCAN THE HORIZON   (~5–10 MIN)

Select and read, listen to, or watch one **article, podcast, or short video outside your usual field**, such as:

- a story of a leader who successfully integrated multiple strategic practices into daily decision-making,
- an analysis of how combining different ways of thinking strengthened an organization's agility,
- a case study of a team that turned strategic thinking into a cultural norm.

Jot a sentence or two: *What lesson does this example give me about sustaining a holistic strategic mindset?*

ASK A STRATEGIC QUESTION   (~5 MIN)

Choose a current project or decision and ask:

"How can I apply at least two of the habits I've practiced (for example: trade-off analysis and scenario thinking) to make this decision stronger?"

Capture your first thoughts, focus on combining habits to enrich your decision-making.

....

....

Whenever a meaningful decision arises, pause briefly:

"Does this action move us closer to where we want to be in 1–3 years?"

Record a quick yes/no or a few words explaining your reasoning.

....

END-OF-DAY CHECK

Circle the word that best describes your mindset tonight:

Clear   Curious   Stretched   Unsure   Energized

STRATEGIC TIP: If you circled *Curious* or *Unsure*, list one resource, an article, a mentor, a short video, you'll explore to help you move toward clarity.

....

REFLECTION PROMPT:

What evidence from today confirms that I am becoming a more strategic thinker, and how can I reinforce that identity daily?

....

....

....

WHY IT MATTERS

Strategic thinking mastery isn't about isolated skills, it's about integrating multiple habits into one seamless way of leading. Today's practice helps you recognize how far you've come and invites you to blend these disciplines into your everyday leadership style.

Day 65 — Mastery & Integration

Practice combining multiple strategic habits, so they become a natural part of your daily leadership approach.

MORNING PROMPT   (~5 MIN)

Pause and write:

"Which decision or project today gives me the best opportunity to apply at least two of the habits I've built such as systems thinking, trade-off analysis, or scenario planning?"

Identify the decision or project and briefly describe how you will use these habits.

....

....

SCAN THE HORIZON   (~5–10 MIN)

Select and read, listen to, or watch one article, **podcast, or short video outside your usual field**, such as:

- a story of a leader who successfully blended several strategic disciplines,
- a case study showing how integrating different thinking styles improved organizational agility,
- an analysis of how cross-disciplinary insight created breakthrough strategy.

Jot a sentence or two: *What does this example teach me about weaving different strategic practices together?*

....

....

ASK A STRATEGIC QUESTION   (~5 MIN)

Choose a current initiative and ask:

"If I deliberately integrate at least two of the habits I've practiced over the past nine weeks, how will it change the quality of my decision or the clarity of my plan?"

Capture your first thoughts, focus on how combined habits improve strategic outcomes.

....

....

STRATEGIC FILTER   (THROUGHOUT THE DAY)

Whenever a meaningful decision arises, pause briefly:

"Does this action move us closer to where we want to be in 1–3 years?"

Record a quick yes/no or a few words explaining your reasoning.

....

END-OF-DAY CHECK

Circle the word that best describes your mindset tonight:

Clear   Curious   Stretched   Unsure   Energized

STRATEGIC TIP: If you circled *Curious* or *Unsure*, list one resource, an article, a mentor, a short video, you'll explore to help you move toward clarity.

....

REFLECTION PROMPT:

Which strategic habit now feels natural to me, and how will I deepen or scale it over the next 90 days?

....

....

....

WHY IT MATTERS

Mastery in strategic thinking means **using multiple disciplines together without even thinking about it**. Today's practice strengthens your ability to combine the habits you've built so that strategic thinking becomes an instinctive part of every decision.

Day 66 — Mastery & Integration

GOAL

Pause to celebrate your progress and commit to sustaining your strategic thinking habits beyond these 66 days.

MORNING PROMPT　　　　　　　　　　　　　　　(~5 MIN)

Pause and write:

"Looking back over the past 66 days, which habit or mindset shift has most transformed my leadership and how will I carry it forward?"

Name the habit or mindset and briefly describe how you will keep it alive in your daily work.

....

....

SCAN THE HORIZON　　　　　　　　　　　　　(~5–10 MIN)

Select and read, listen to, or watch one article, **podcast, or short video outside your usual field**, such as:

- a story of a leader who turned a 90-day challenge into a lasting cultural shift,
- an analysis of how daily strategic habits became an organization's competitive edge,
- a reflection on sustaining growth and learning over the long term.

Jot a sentence or two: What does this example teach me about making strategic thinking a permanent part of leadership?

....

....

ASK A STRATEGIC QUESTION　　　　　　　　　(~5 MIN)

Choose a current priority or decision and ask:

"How will I intentionally keep these strategic habits, future focus, systems thinking, pattern recognition, scenario planning, and influential communication, alive over the next 90 days?"

　　　　　　　　　　　　　　　　　　　　

Capture your first thoughts; these will form the foundation of your personal 90-day continuation plan.

....

....

STRATEGIC FILTER   (THROUGHOUT THE DAY)

Whenever a meaningful decision arises, pause briefly:

"Does this action move us closer to where we want to be in 1–3 years?"

Record a quick yes/no or a few words explaining your reasoning.

....

END-OF-DAY CHECK

Circle the word that best describes your mindset tonight:

Clear   Curious   Stretched   Unsure   Energized

STRATEGIC TIP: If you circled *Curious* or *Unsure*, list one resource, an article, a mentor, a short video, you'll explore to help you move toward clarity.

....

REFLECTION PROMPT:

Looking ahead, what is the one strategic commitment I will carry forward, and what support, structure, or cadence will keep it alive?

....

....

....

WHY IT MATTERS

Strategic thinking mastery is not an endpoint, it's a **lifelong practice**. By pausing to recognize your growth and plan for the next 90 days, you ensure the habits you've built become a natural, enduring part of how you lead.

Final Strategic Challenge – Sustaining Strategic Habits

SCENARIO:

You've completed the 66-day journey and developed a powerful set of strategic habits. Now, real life resumes with deadlines, meetings, and urgent demands.

YOUR TASK:

1. Repeat the Strategic Intelligence Assessment that follows. Note the differences.

2. Identify the **three habits** from this journal that you refuse to let slip.

3. List two structures of accountability you will put in place (for example: a monthly check-in with a coach or peer, a recurring calendar reminder, or a short weekly journal entry).

4. Draft a personal commitment statement describing how you will keep strategic thinking alive in your leadership for the next 90 days.

REFLECT:

- Which daily practices felt most natural and sustainable?
- Where will you need extra support or accountability?
- What difference do you already notice in how you lead?

To keep sharpening your strategic thinking, explore additional scenarios in the **ThinkSuite™ Strategic Intelligence Decks™** *or schedule a* **Strategic Conversation™** *with a coach to deepen your growth in the next phase.*

Strategic Intelligence Self-(re)Assessment

It's time to measure your growth as a strategic thinker.

INSTRUCTIONS

For each statement below, rate how true it is for you **today**:

1 = Not true **3** = Occasionally true **5** = Very true

2 = Seldom true **4** = Often true

LENS 1: CLARITY – Seeing the Big Picture

1. I deliberately step back to understand the broader context before making decisions.
2. I connect daily actions to my long-term goals and organizational strategy.
3. I can clearly explain the trends, forces, or data shaping my environment.
4. I look beyond immediate problems to uncover underlying patterns.
5. I regularly pause to test whether my work aligns with the outcomes that matter most.

LENS 2: CONFIDENCE – Thinking Boldly and Deciding with Courage

1. I make decisions even when information is incomplete or ambiguous.
2. I trust my ability to weigh options and anticipate second-order effects.
3. I invite diverse viewpoints, then confidently synthesize them into a clear direction.
4. I stay grounded and composed when strategic choices carry high stakes.
5. I recover quickly when a decision doesn't play out as expected and adjust with focus.

1. I translate strategic ideas into concrete actions that move key priorities forward.
2. I influence stakeholders outside my immediate team or department.
3. I build alliances that help execute long-range plans.
4. I can point to outcomes that reflect thoughtful, forward-looking decisions.
5. I mentor or coach others to strengthen their own strategic thinking.

SCORING & REFLECTION

- Add the scores for each lens (range 5–25).
- Compare the total from Day 1 to now; this is how you've progressed over 66 days.
- After rating yourself, capture:

1. How have I strategically grown?

2. When did I retreat into short-term or reactive thinking?

3. What single shift most improved my strategic thinking during the prior 66 days?

Incorporate your findings into the strategic review below.

66-Day Strategic Review

Integration. Insight. Identity.

You've completed 66 days of intentional strategic practice. This is your moment to pause, honor the work, and integrate the mindset shifts, habits, and clarity you've gained.

This review is not about perfection, it's about **pattern recognition, strategic self-awareness, and conscious evolution**. Use these prompts to capture who you've become and who you're ready to be next.

1. What Are the Most Significant Wins from the Last 66 Days?

Include accomplishments, decisions, habits, mindset shifts, breakthroughs, or moments of clarity.

....

....

....

2. What Challenges Did I Face, and How Did I Grow Through Them?

Reflect on patterns of resistance, overwhelm, drift, or hesitation, and how you overcame them.

....

....

....

3. What Patterns Do I Now Recognize in My Thinking or Behavior?

Note recurring habits, triggers, strengths, or barriers that showed up across the journey.

....

....

....

4. How Has My Strategic Thinking Changed Since Day 1?

After repeating the Strategic Intelligence Assessment, consider how your clarity, prioritization, discipline, emotional regulation, long-term focus, and decision-making have improved.

5. What Habits or Practices Were Most Impactful?

Identify the routines, rituals, or tools you want to carry forward.

6. What Did I Learn About My Capacity, Leadership, or Identity?

This is where deep self-awareness emerges.

7. What Needs to Continue? What Needs to Stop? What Needs to be Refined?

Continue:

Stop:

Refine:

8. How Will I Sustain Strategic Thinking Beyond These 66 Days?

List 1–3 commitments or systems that will help you maintain momentum.

9. My Strategic Identity Statement

Summarize the leader you have become because of completing this journey.

"I am a leader who…"

10. My Strategic Commitment for the Next 66 Days

Choose one clear, compelling commitment that carries your strategic growth forward.

My Commitment:

CLOSING REFLECTION

"What is now possible for me that wasn't possible 66 days ago?"

Write your answer with confidence and clarity:

Notes

Pause and Reflect

Congratulations, you've completed **66 Days to Strategic Thinking**. I know it has not been easy; growth never is. But you made it regardless of whether it was 66, 99, or 120+ days. You. Made. It.

Over the past weeks, you have paused with intention, trained your mind to see patterns and possibilities, and built habits that will shape the way you lead for years to come.

But this is not the end.

Strategic thinking is a lifelong practice. The real impact begins as you carry these habits back into your daily leadership:

- Keep asking future-focused questions before making decisions.
- Continue scanning the horizon for signals and patterns that others may miss.
- Invite your team into the conversation so that strategic thinking becomes a shared culture.
- Revisit your notes often; this journal can become a trusted playbook whenever you need clarity.

Consider setting a 90-day calendar reminder to check back on the commitments you recorded on **Day 66**.

And if you want to keep your growth momentum strong, explore the companion resources, **ThinkSuite™ Strategic Intelligence Decks™**, **Strategic Conversations™**, or a personalized coaching engagement.

Pause. Think. Grow. Strategically.™ isn't a slogan, it's a way of leading.

When you practice it, you transform your prior conditioning into one that will serve now and well into your future, and the more naturally you will inspire others to do the same.

About Pamela J. Green

Pamela J. Green is an internationally recognized executive coach, strategist, and leadership advisor with more than 30 years of experience guiding senior leaders and boards through complex challenges.

Consistently named one of Washington, D.C.'s Top 20 Coaches, Pam blends board-level strategy, organizational development, and executive coaching to help leaders pause intentionally, think strategically, and grow their influence.

She is the founder of Pamela J. Green Solutions, LLC and the creator of the ThinkSuite™ ecosystem, an integrated suite of tools and experiences that includes the ThinkSuite™ Studio, Strategic Intelligence DecksTM, and Strategic Conversations™.

Pam is the author of the acclaimed Think Like a Brand® and Think Like an Executive Brand® books, which inspire leaders to craft influential personal and organizational brands. She holds a Bachelor of Science and MBA from Franklin University in Columbus, Ohio, and is currently completing her Ph.D. in Organizational Leadership.

Her professional certifications include Professional Certified Coach (PCC) from the International Coach Federation, SPHR from the Human Resource Certification Institute (HRCI), and Internal Conflict Coach (ICC).

Through her keynotes, executive retreats, coaching programs, and thought leadership, Pamela J. Green equips executives, aspiring C-suite leaders, and executive teams to create clarity, confidence, and impact in an increasingly complex world.

Connect and learn more at **pamelajgreen.com**.

Strategic Questions & Strategic Filters: A Leadership Reference Guide

These questions are the backbone of strategic thinking. Use these questions and filters when decisions feel complex, urgent, or politically charged. You don't need all of them; one well-chosen question can change the trajectory of a conversation.

STRATEGIC FILTERS

Use these questions in real time, before, during, or immediately after a decision.

1. Does this align with where we want to be in 1–3 years?
2. Does this move us closer to where we want to be in 1–3 years?
3. Does this action keep us aligned with where we want to be in 1–3 years?
4. Does this choice move us closer to where we want to be in 1–3 years?

The intentional repetition reinforces habit formation and embeds a single strategic "throughline" across decisions of all sizes.

STRATEGIC QUESTIONS

These are the core questions practiced throughout the 66-day journey. They are grouped here for fast access and reuse.

Future Focus & Long-Range Thinking

1. What does success look like in one year?
2. What would success look like in three years?
3. If this were wildly successful in three years, what would have to be true?
4. What outcome do I most want to protect or achieve over the next 1–3 years?
5. How does today shape tomorrow?

Risk, Assumptions & Blind Spots

6. What might get in our way?

7. What's a possible unintended consequence?
8. What risk are we not talking about?
9. If nothing changes in our environment over the next year, what risk might we be overlooking?
10. If we do nothing differently for the next year, what unintended consequences might arise?
11. Which assumption I'm holding might deserve to be questioned?
12. If our key assumption proves wrong, what would we need to change—immediately and over the next year?

Opportunity & Strategic Advantage

13. What hidden opportunity could this challenge reveal?
14. If this initiative succeeds beyond expectations, what will we need to have in place to sustain it?
15. If this initiative were to exceed expectations, what new challenges might we face a year from now?
16. If we approached this challenge from the perspective of a competitor or outsider, what opportunity would they see that we don't?

Perspective-Shifting & Reframing

17. If someone with no stake in this decision were advising us, what question would they ask first?
18. What big decision or challenge would benefit from a powerful question rather than a quick answer?
19. What decision or issue might benefit from a completely different perspective?

Strategic Resilience & Adaptation

20. If our most important long-term goal suddenly became much harder to reach, what would we need to rethink right now?
21. If this emerging signal proves significant, what early moves should we consider?
22. If we suddenly had to double the impact of this work in the next year, what would need to change today?

Integration & Reflection

23. Looking back, which strategic question sparked the biggest insight—and why?
24. What does the strategic version of me need next week?

References

Duke, A. (2018). *Thinking in Bets: Making smarter decisions when you don't have all the facts*. Portfolio.

Kahneman, D., Sibony, O., & Sunstein, C. R. (2021). *Noise: A flaw in human judgment*. Little, Brown Spark.

Lafley, A. G., & Martin, R. L. (2013). *Playing to Win: How strategy really works*. Harvard Business Review Press.

Lally, P., Van Jaarsveld, C. H. M., Potts, H. W. W., & Wardle, J. (2010). How are habits formed: Modelling habit formation in the real world. *European Journal of Social Psychology, 40*(6), 998–1009.

Meadows, D. H. (2008). *Thinking in Systems: A primer*. Chelsea Green Publishing.

McKeown, G. (2014). *Essentialism: The disciplined pursuit of less*. Crown Business.

Newport, C. (2016). *Deep Work: Rules for focused success in a distracted world*. Grand Central Publishing.

Rumelt, R. (2011). *Good Strategy Bad Strategy: The difference and why it matters*. Crown Business.

Schein, E. H. (2010). *Organizational Culture and Leadership* (4th ed.). Jossey-Bass.

www.ingramcontent.com/pod-product-compliance
Lightning Source LLC
Chambersburg PA
CBHW050026040726
47599CB00015B/1554